With over a hundred languages spoken daily in Greater London, cross-cultural awareness for effective Christian communication is no longer a mere optional extra. Whether we live and minister in Birmingham, Bradford or Blantyre, it is now quite simply essential. Added to this is a second major challenge highlighted by Jonathan Groves – "The rapid growth of the church in Malawi has far outstripped the ability of African theological institutions and correspondence courses to supply trained church leaders". Groves has brought together these dual global challenges in a book that takes serious account of the three horizons of biblical interpretation. The sheer richness and relevance of Romans are revealed, often in new and unexpected ways, as Groves pays careful attention to the role of text and context at each horizon. The Word and Spirit of God will bring true change in church and society through the use of the hermeneutical approaches presented in this timely book. Dedicated and determined teachers and preachers will benefit hugely from this highly significant and exciting study of the one Pauline letter that we all thought we knew inside out!

Dr Derek Newton
former MTh Programme leader
International Christian College, Scotland

The engagement of the peoples of Africa with the biblical text is both vast in extent and profound in depth. No one can fully understand sub-Saharan Africa today without some appreciation of the role of the Bible in the life of society. Equally no one can claim a comprehensive knowledge of contemporary biblical interpretation without paying serious attention to the use of the Bible in African communities. Greatly needed therefore are sophisticated and detailed studies like Jonathan Groves' analysis of the interpretation of Paul's letter to the Romans in the context of provincial-rural Malawi. This is a pioneering and important contribution to our understanding both of the Book of Romans and of grassroots biblical hermeneutics in the African context.

Kenneth R. Ross
formerly Professor of Theology
University of Malawi

D0279893

Global Perspectives Series

Reading Romans at Ground Level

Langham
GLOBAL LIBRARY

Reading Romans at Ground Level

A Contemporary Rural African Perspective

Jonathan D. Groves

Foreword by David W. Smith

© 2015 by Jonathan D. Groves

Published 2015 by Langham Global Library
an imprint of Langham Creative Projects

Langham Partnership
PO Box 296, Carlisle, Cumbria CA3 9WZ, UK
www.langham.org

ISBNs:
978-1-783689-20-0 Print
978-1-783689-18-7 Mobi
978-1-783689-19-4 ePub
978-1-78368-875-3 PDF

British Library Cataloguing in Publication Data

Groves, Jonathan D., author.
 Reading Romans at ground level : a contemporary African
 perspective.
 1. Bible. Romans--Study and teaching--Malawi. 2. Church
 work--Malawi. 3. Christian life--Malawi.
 I. Title
 227.1'0071'06897-dc23

 ISBN-13: 9781783689200

Cover & Book Design: projectluz.com

CONTENTS

Foreword

This study of Paul's epistle to the Romans combines wide knowledge of contemporary Western scholarship on this letter with a sensitive awareness of the context of African believers in rural Malawi, and it moves skilfully between these very different situations in the effort to create hermeneutical bridges between them. At the same time, the author is deeply aware of the influence of a third culture, that of the modern Western world, both on himself and on the European missionaries who first announced the message of Christ to traditional African peoples. This work is clearly motivated by a deep concern that the Bible might be liberated from received traditions of interpretation when they inhibit its transformative power in contexts of great poverty, suffering and oppression. Underpinning this desire is an evident sense of respect, fellowship and concern for those African Christians whose lives are lived in an uneasy conversation between their traditional worldview, their faith in Jesus, and the ever-encroaching culture of Western modernity. Jonathan Groves has reflected at length on the challenges thrown up by this situation and his resultant study is a pioneering piece of work which may be said to break fresh ground in contextual and inter-cultural theology.

The specific ideas suggested here with regard to points of contact between the Pauline gospel and the concrete pastoral and ethical dilemmas facing contemporary African believers reveal the writer's serious engagement with the church in Malawi and his understanding of its specific religious and cultural context. At the same time, he is obviously abreast of current debates in New Testament studies in the academy and handles areas of disagreement over the recent scholarly interpretation of the letter to the Romans with wisdom and insight.

The most significant aspect of this work concerns the discovery of surprising connections between the context of the first hearers of this letter in the slums of the imperial city of ancient Rome and that of poor Christians in the contemporary setting of rural Africa. These correspondences provide rural Malawian believers with the possibility of insight into the meaning of many texts, meanings which remain hidden from prosperous and comfortable readers in the Global North whose material circumstances are so utterly different from those of *both* the original receptors of Paul's letter, and poor

Christians living on the underside of the process of globalization today. In the following pages Groves makes excellent use of Peter Oakes' illuminating reconstruction of a primitive Christian community, living and meeting in the squalid and dangerous tenement blocks in first century Rome, which first heard this letter read. Indeed, this present study exemplifies Oakes' conclusion that, while there is a place for academic theorizing about the complexities of Paul's greatest epistle, "there is also a place for thinking about how it sounds to people at ground level" (Oakes 2009, 179).

It is my conviction, discussed in detail elsewhere (Smith 2013, 120–150), that we are on the brink of a radical change in the interpretation and pastoral and missiological application of the letter to the Romans. The emergence of world Christianity, with its heartlands located among the poor and deprived across the Global South, is creating an entirely new historical and cultural context within which Paul, and indeed the rest of the New Testament, is being heard, taught and discussed today. This context, very often urban in character, and frequently shaped by life in the ever-growing slums of the exploding cities of the southern continents, inevitably spawns new and urgent questions which are brought to the text, and which require answers if faith is to remain credible for people whose daily existence is often marked by a struggle between life and death. What is remarkable and wonderfully exciting is the realization that these very issues are far from remote to the purpose and content of Paul's letter. Addressed to "all in Rome who are loved by God and called to be saints", this letter challenges the idolatry and gross injustice of an empire which boasted that it was the agent of a universal *gospel*, while it condemned the mass of humankind to poverty and servitude. It is precisely such people, humiliated and degraded, who are assured of God's unconditional love, so that those without respect and honour in Roman society gain a new status and find in the *gospel of God* a firm basis for human dignity and hope. As Robert Jewett says in his ground-breaking commentary on this letter, Paul's claim that salvation comes through Christ crucified and risen undermines the Roman propaganda which "filled the city to which this letter was addressed", and his insistence that the divine righteousness revealed through the Cross overturned the system of shame and honour upon which the Empire rested, means that Paul's letter "effectively turns the social value system of the Roman Empire upside down" (Jewett 2007, 138–139).

Jonathan Groves' research reveals that African pastors in rural Malawi found Paul's letter to be difficult and struggled to see its relevance to their situation beyond certain favoured texts. The great merit of his work is that it opens up connections between those two worlds in ways that are exciting and creative. However, as the inexorable pressure of urbanization grows throughout the African continent, weakening the hold of traditional religion and driving the young into the cities, the meaning of Romans will be further illuminated and it will come to be recognized as a crucial resource for the liberation and freedom of the human family which the gospel promises. Thus, the book you hold in your hands represents the cutting edge of biblical interpretation in the globalized world of the twenty-first century, but it is merely the harbinger of a coming transformation in the life and mission of Christianity, which, please God, may exceed anything we can imagine at the present time.

David W. Smith
Lecturer on Mission in the Contemporary World
Irish Bible Institute, Dublin

Preface

This book uses a three-horizon contextual approach to 'read' the Letter to the Romans in the context of provincial-rural Malawi. Padilla (1981, 18) observed: "The contextual approach recognizes both the role of the ancient world in shaping the original text and the role of today's world in conditioning the way contemporary readers are likely to 'hear' and understand the text." Giving consideration to three-horizons helps to recognise the distinct yet interactive roles of authors, interpreters and audiences in the creation of meaning.

Thiselton (1980, 103) argued: "Understanding takes place when two sets of horizons are brought into relation to each other, namely those of the text and those of the interpreter." Yet when the final audience occupies an acutely different (cross-cultural) context from that of the interpreter, three-horizons must be considered (Carson 1984, 17). This perspective is foundational to this study. Field research in Malawi and literature analysis has affirmed there are chasms to bridge between the past context of the text and the contemporary contexts of interpreter and audience.

This work seeks to combine historical, cultural and hermeneutical dimensions to gain insight into how Romans might be understood and used in rural Malawi. It maintains, "every truth from God comes in cultural guise" (Carson 1984, 19), and hence no interpretation can ever be entirely free from culture-based presuppositions. This reading of Romans is a product of the interface between the first-horizon of ancient Rome and the natural third-horizon of contemporary rural Malawi, but with interferences from all mediating second-horizons, including the Western interpreter – the author of this book.

Abstract

This book uses a three-horizon contextual approach to interpret the Letter to the Romans in the context of rural Malawi. Field research was conducted with serving pastors and lay leaders from town and village congregations, both evangelical and Pentecostal, at two towns in Central and Southern Malawi. Using questionnaires, interviews and observations from Malawi, and analysis of the literature, a profile was developed of an under-trained church leadership facing a range of socio-cultural and pastoral issues. This profile was used as a model for the contemporary third-horizon context of rural Malawi.

Aspects of the original first-horizon context of ancient Rome were provisionally reconstructed from the literature. This perspective was then combined with the model third-horizon to produce a 'reading' of Romans in rural Malawi that was culturally and historically-informed. In their existing use of Romans many sermons quoted one of five highly popular verses/verse-pairs (1:16–17; 3:23; 6:23; 10:9–10 and 12:1–2), typically as part of a simple gospel presentation to secure new converts and assert Christian identity in the community. Sermons often quoted prominent theological words interpreted literally and without contextualisation. Complete paragraphs were used less commonly in preaching, but were generally topical, inductive responses to felt needs, sometimes using radical reader response. The study presents examples of theologically rich contextual readings of Romans which engage with the socio-cultural and pastoral problems of Malawian life, and it considers the impact of second-horizon interferences upon the natural Malawian third-horizon.

Acknowledgments

This book is based upon my dissertation at International Christian College, Glasgow, UK. It was submitted in partial fulfilment of the Master of Theology in Biblical Interpretation of the University of Aberdeen, UK. I wish to thank Pastor Michael-John Phiri, Principal of the Evangelical Bible College of Malawi, Blantyre, for inviting me to the two Pastors' and Elders' Book Conferences held at Liwonde and Mponela, and for granting permission to carry out my field research there. I also thank the former Director of Zambesi Mission, Mr Jim Hasnip, for his help and support in making this possible.

Special thanks are due to all the Malawian church leaders who so willingly provided me with the data about their ministries. I also thank the following for help with the field research: Pastor Bright Gama, Mr Eddie Mubengo and Mr Jonathan Stephens for reviewing the questionnaire and interview sheets; Pastor Robert Yanduya, Pastor Innocent Wachimwa and Pastor Connex Ijalasi for providing support to the participants at the Conferences; Pastor Yanduya, Pastor Wachimwa and Pastor Gama for translating into English those questionnaires that were returned in Chichewa; and Pastor Gama for setting up the Contextual Bible studies.

I thank my supervisor, Dr Ronnie Sim for helpful suggestions and feedback. Finally, I thank my family Ruth, Rachel and Timothy for their unwavering love and patience with me.

1

Introduction

1.1 Research Questions

This work uses field data collected at rural locations in Central and Southern Malawi to help address the following research questions:

1. What are the socio-cultural and pastoral issues experienced by church leaders in provincial-rural Malawi?

2. How is the Letter to the Romans currently used and interpreted in provincial-rural Malawi?

3. How might Romans be used in the context of provincial-rural Malawi to address these socio-cultural and pastoral issues?

The term 'provincial-rural' is used to signify provincial market towns and rural villages – everywhere away from the main urban centres. In the long-term, the study aspires to assist with the design of contextual Bible training for provincial-rural church leaders who have previously lacked any such opportunity.

The rest of this chapter introduces the educational, cultural, ecclesiastical, hermeneutical and kerygmatic contexts of provincial-rural Malawi, and the choice of Romans as a model letter for this study.

1.2 Educational Context: Need for Biblically Trained Leaders

Malawi is a densely populated country in Central Africa with little development and an economy that is highly dependent upon agriculture (Mandryk 2010, 552). The majority of its 14 million population live in provincial-rural locations where education levels are generally much lower than in the major cities of Blantyre and Lilongwe. While the Christian church has seen unparalleled numerical growth in Malawi over the past half century, the consequences for discipleship in rural congregations are daunting.

The US Centre for World Missions estimates there are two million untrained 'functional pastors' leading churches in the world today (USCWM, 2007). The lack of culturally sensitive, affordable theological training in the non-Western world has been a concern for decades. Clause 11 of the Lausanne Covenant (Lausanne, 1974) stated:

> We recognize that there is a great need to improve theological education, especially for church leaders. In every nation and culture there should be an effective training program for pastors and laity in doctrine, discipleship, evangelism, nurture and service.

In Malawi, churches and prayer houses continue to be planted throughout the country by both missionary- and African-initiated denominations. The number of pastors, lay elders and women's ministry leaders in Bible teaching or preaching ministries probably runs into tens of thousands. It is estimated that up to 90 percent of such church leaders have received little or no formal theological training (Ijalasi, 2011), and that 95 percent of pastors are not seminary educated (SIM, 2012).

Literacy levels in rural Malawi are patchy and it is uncertain how well those possessing vernacular Bibles can actually read or understand them (Kalilombe 1999, 196–199). Untrained pastors may themselves have little idea how to use the Bible for discipleship. Mijoga (2000,13) comments that "most 'readers' of the Bible in Malawi are non-literate", if 'readers' includes the many who listen to, discuss and retell the Bible, without an ability to read for themselves.

1.3   Cultural Context: African Traditional Religion and Worldview

Presuppositions from the traditional African worldview fundamentally shape religious and cultural thinking at all levels of Malawian society, especially in provincial-rural locations. It is important therefore to identify the key aspects of African cultural beliefs; contrast them with external Western thought patterns; and assess their impact upon Biblical interpretation and preaching in Malawi.

First, Malawians are in general profoundly spiritual people. Monotheism is not a new idea throughout sub-Saharan Africa: the concept of God is indigenous, not imported (Bediako, 1995; Kärkkäinen 2003, 246). Long before Christianity arrived, African Traditional Religion (ATR) recognized the existence of a 'Supreme Being' who is creator of all things and source of all life and strength (Bujo 1992, 17; VanBreugel 2001, 29–34). He is mysterious, self-sufficient and has the highest rank in the visible and invisible worlds. The attributes and activities of this Supreme Being have traditionally been understood from innumerable tribal myths which seek to explain both prehistory and history (Mbiti 1989, 23; VanBreugel 2001, 35–38; Wendland & Hachibamba 2007, 71–107). Like Paul preaching in Athens (Acts 17:23–24), many of the pioneer Christian missionaries re-appropriated this 'unknown god' into their own gospel proclamation.

Mateyu (2011), a Malawian Bible College lecturer, affirms that in Malawi today: "The existence of God (*Mulungu*) is unquestionable . . . It is a given belief that is taught to all children. He is self-existent and creator of all things. However, he is a supreme spirit, not personal." Although eternal, omniscient and omnipotent, this 'Supreme Being' is remote; he withdrew from the world after mankind disappointed him, and does not communicate with people directly. People may seek to make contact with him through their recently deceased ancestors (Mbiti 1989, 26) who acquire a supernatural status enabling them to act as potential mediators (Kärkkäinen 2003, 249) and can act as intercessors (VanBreugel 2001, 38–41). Ancestral spirits are considered as living and active members of the family with a role to play in maintaining the harmony and morality of the community (Wendland & Hachibamba 2007, 168–169; VanBreugel 2001, 73–83). In an unpredictable world where health and prosperity are vulnerable, their sympathetic intervention is sought. Traditional village life is beset by fear at every level, and there is a deep need for liberation (Msiska 1996, 71–72).

Second, African worldview sees God, humanity, spirits and the cosmos as a single interconnected whole. Human birth, life and death comprise a rhythm of nature marked by a succession of initiation rites and life transitions; death is merely a change of state. The material and spiritual, visible and invisible, sacred and profane, together comprise a unified reality, often shaped by experiences of suffering and fear. It is unusual to compartmentalize reality (Dada 2010, 160). In Malawi, the material and spiritual are considered to be in constant interaction, events in the one affecting the other (Van der Meer 2011, 78–79).

In the traditional worldview many evil spiritual forces threaten human wellbeing. They exert their supernatural powers through men and women who work in allegiance with them to perform witchcraft (VanBreugel 2001, 211–231), causing much popular fear of disease, misfortune or death (Dicks 2012, 102). There are also socially acceptable forms of magic, such as traditional medicine, in which the 'magicians' of the community invoke higher powers to protect people or property from misfortune (VanBreugel 2001, 246–254).

Mbiti (1975, 165) says:

> People believe there are invisible, mystical forces and powers in the universe. It is also believed that certain human beings have a knowledge and ability of how to tap, control and use these forces . . . Magic is believed to be these forces in the hands of certain individuals . . . They may use magic for harmful ends, and then people experience it as bad or evil magic. Or they may use it for ends which are helpful to society, and then it is considered as good magic or 'medicine'.

In contrast, the Western modernist outlook tends to rationalize life events, compartmentalizing reality into physical, emotional and spiritual components. Many Western missionaries in Malawi have therefore denied the existence of evil spirits and magic, trivializing African fears of witchcraft and use of traditional medicine, and rejecting that such magic is of any consequence. Van der Meer (2011, 80) comments:

> Unfortunately, this approach did not meet the pastoral need of the African believers, who urgently sought deliverance from what they perceived as harassment by evil spirits, curses, and witchcraft. As Christianity did not appear to have a solution for the problem of witchcraft, many Africans continued to seek assistance from the traditional healers and diviners. In spite of improved education and continuing church growth in Africa, witchcraft is one of the most enduring and pervasive elements of African traditional religion in the twenty-first century.

Other Western missionaries (coming from Pentecostal traditions) have taken the spiritual reality underlying magic and witchcraft more seriously. Although this has been more pastorally relevant in Africa than the modernist approach, by tending to label almost all African traditional practices as demonic the underlying issues behind witchcraft have often remained unaddressed.

Indeed, by creating a close association between traditional African spirits and personalized demons, they may actually have authenticated belief in the power of witchcraft. Van der Meer (2011, 80–81) says: "We must heed Paul Hiebert's caution that while taking the power of the evil supernatural seriously, we must also guard against Christianity itself being adapted into a new form of magic." It is easy for traditional beliefs and Christian spiritual warfare to blend into a dangerous medieval cocktail of demonology and witch-hunting[1] that stands far from Biblical Christianity (Van der Meer 2010, 166). The majority of deaths are still attributed to witchcraft. "Even Christians, in times of stress, frequently revert to behaviour inspired by fear of witchcraft" (VanBreugel 2001, 211). Pre-occupation with witchcraft beliefs thus present serious pastoral problems for the church in Malawi, and pastors frequently struggle to implement a contextual, yet Biblically faithful response.

Third, African tradition holds to a holistic and community centred view of life. It seeks earthly happiness and harmony. Mbiti (1989, 110) sums this up: "I am, because we are." The African focus is upon practical and experiential redemption through "personal and community deliverance from the forces of evil, witchcraft, death, drought, floods, sickness or any epidemic" (Appiah–Kubi 1987, 72). Communally, they seek to counter their deep-rooted sense of vulnerability. African contextual Bible readings may become dialogues primarily between text and community, rather than text and individual (LeMarquand 2005, 32) as is typically so in the West. They see God intervening pragmatically to rescue people, but not especially as 'the One' who atones for sin. The proclamation of a gospel in which Christ provides personal forgiveness from sin through his sacrificial death on the cross is perceived by many as an overly individualistic Western thought-form (Stinton 2004, 34). In summary, Africans can relate to the idea of God, but may have difficulty with contextualizing Jesus.

1.4   Ecclesiastical Context: The Church in Malawi

The church in Malawi today can generally be divided into two main groupings, according to their origins. These are the mainstream or missionary-initiated denominations, and the African-instituted, independent or indigenous churches (AICs). The institutional mainstream churches (Presbyterian, Anglican, Roman Catholic) were established in Malawi out of the early

---

1. In 2008, witch-hunts in Malawi led to the torture and murder of many suspects.

Colonial missions in the late nineteenth century. They brought with them the theology and practices of their Western founders. Missionary-instituted Pentecostals (Assemblies of God) arrived in Malawi by the mid-twentieth century. Religious independency in Malawi has developed progressively from missionary foundations throughout the twentieth century. Change was driven forward fastest during key times of political (1900–1919) and social protest (1923–1935) and of religious renewal (1969–1978) when many new indigenous Pentecostal movements were born.

There are two views on the causal origin and growth of the AICs within Malawi (Mijoga 1996, 362). The first is negative – that they emerged as breakaways from mainstream Christianity as a result of its failure to meet the needs and aspirations of Malawians. Mbiti (1986, 16) wrote:

> Many of these independent churches separated themselves from mission churches, and others from one another, largely in protest over some form or another of authority, or in order to find fulfilment of a spiritual thirst outside of the mission form of Christianity.

Typically, the catalyst for action was the emergence of an influential 'prophet' figure. From this perspective, the AICs in Malawi could be viewed as protest movements seeking religious liberation from oppressive structures within the missionary churches (Mijoga 2000, 174).

The second view is more positive – that AICs arose spontaneously as an "attempt by Malawian Christians to apply the resources of the Scripture to their own life in their own time and place" (Chakanza 1982, 133). Doing theology within Malawi necessitates relating Christian faith and traditional culture. While retaining most of the doctrines of the missionary churches, the AICs have adopted traditional practices such as storytelling, singing and dancing, apparently borrowing heavily from their own culture. Mbiti (1986, 17) wrote:

> In a large number of cases, independent churches have evolved concrete forms of Christian life, both in thought and practice, which incorporate more genuine African elements than do many mission churches, in the sense of integrating the Christian message into the indigenous culture and problems of the people.

To varying degrees, the AICs may therefore have been influenced by the beliefs and practices of ATR in an attempt to increase the relevance of Christianity to ordinary Malawians (Mijoga 1996, 359). Access to vernacular Bibles gave

Africans a new level of control over interpreting the Scriptures, so allowing them to critique the readings given to them by the missionaries on issues like polygamy and ancestors (Barratt 1968, 127–129). Practical disputes over money, alcohol, leadership and divorce were also driving forces for change, more than doctrinal differences (Mijoga 1996, 360).

1.5   Hermeneutical Context: African Biblical Interpretation

The rapid growth of the church in Malawi has far outstripped the ability of African theological institutions and correspondence courses to supply trained church leaders. The need is most acute amongst provincial-rural churches where few churches can afford to support their leaders at all (Mandryk 2010, 37; 2010, 554).

The majority of church leaders in Malawi have received little or no formal instruction in how to 'read' their Bibles. They interpret Scripture literally and uncritically (as intuitively do many people in the UK too), without considering the classic three-ways of reading (Vanhoozer 1998, 19–23):

1) The socio-historical setting 'behind' the text.

2) The literary characteristics and genre 'inside' the text.

3) The reader's own situation 'in front of' the text.

Preaching in Malawi is generally of type (3), using inductive reader-response, without consideration of audience, context or canon. Some may indeed consider critical responses to the Bible made on cultural grounds as sinful (Kanyoro 1999, 20).

Today, there are broadly two academic readings of the Bible in Malawi. First, there are the Western-style interpretations. These largely reflect the Enlightenment worldview and religio-cultural practices of the Western colonial missionaries who first brought the gospel to Africa. The prevailing models of African theological education continue to follow this frame of reference through pre-packaged theologies, ethical systems and pastoral methods imported directly from the West (Naidoo 2010, 348). These historical-critical and literary-critical perspectives continue to find praxis within the mainstream institutional denominations especially.

Second, there are the specifically African types of interpretation which have developed since the 1930s in parallel with political and religious independence. Harmony and meaning is traditionally determined in community by listening to old and new interpretative voices, and allowing new interpretations to emerge dynamically from the ensuing conversation (Waweru 2006, 334). The missionaries had failed to recognise this, silencing the 'ungodly' voice of Africans and their culture, and substituting their own Western voices of Christendom by default.

The encounter between the Bible and the African religious and cultural context became increasingly proactive in the 1970s–1990s. African theologians contended "that the culture of the readers has more influence on how the Bible is understood and used than historical facts about the text" (Kanyoro 1999, 20). Particular attention was therefore given to beliefs in ancestors, the spirits, demon possession, witchcraft, sickness and suffering. Evaluative studies were undertaken "to facilitate the communication of the biblical message within the African milieu, and to evolve a new understanding of Christianity that would be African and biblical" (Ukpong 2000, 16).

Since the 1990s, the interaction of Bible and African culture has become more assertive and theologically original. Ordinary Africans (not just scholars) have engaged increasingly with the Bible from within their own holistic worldview, not just through the spectacles of geographical or ideological Westerners. They have sought to relate the Scriptures to the contemporary African social, religious and cultural context. This includes traumatic human situations like poverty, suffering, HIV/AIDS and death. The focus of interpretation has shifted to the *theological* meaning of the Bible, appropriated by linking the text to the contemporary African context (West 2008, 4). Ukpong (2000, 25) commented of contextual approaches: "Their point of departure is the context of the *reader*, and they are all concerned with linking the biblical text to the reader's context." Here, meaning is firmly positioned within the three-cornered hat of the text, the reader and their current context. Successful contextualisation is thus dynamic, demanding that the reader has a firm grasp of both text and social context. Significantly different meanings can be ascribed depending upon the occasion in which the text is read. Such contextual methodologies have found a home among many of the AICs in Malawi.

In response to this hermeneutical paradigm shift, African theological education needs a curriculum that is appropriate for the African context (Nyende 2009, 136). It needs to discover alternative teaching models that are Biblically oriented, yet rooted primarily within African indigenous culture, identity and understanding. Naidoo (2010, 360) comments:

> The theology taught in African theological institutions must give attention to the historical, biblical and pastoral dimensions within

their context in order to have relevance. It begins with theology education, develops contextual approaches and hermeneutical methods like the hermeneutics of inculturation or liberation based on the way African people conceive and interpret reality. It must be supported by tools from African culture like language, art, oral traditions and an African worldview.

In summary, contemporary African hermeneutics would seem to offer no single meaning to a text that may be recovered through historical-critical analysis. Hence, the discovery of meaning and its application to a particular context, are not two successive processes; rather they are viewed by Africans as part-and-parcel of the *same* reader-driven process. As Ukpong (2002, 17) says, "African readings are existential and pragmatic in nature, and contextual in approach . . . and lay no claim to a universal perspective". This assertion is assessed in the conclusion of this book.

1.6   Kerygmatic Context: Preaching in Malawi

This section reviews previous field studies of preaching in Malawi, though each was conducted over 15 years ago. These examined the theology, application of Scripture, and preaching methods in mainstream and independent churches. The work of Ross, Wendland and Mijoga made particular reference to Bible use and interpretation, cultural engagement and audience response.

a)   Mainstream Denominations

During 1990–1992, Ross (1995a) looked at preaching across Malawi in three mainstream missionary-initiated denominations (Presbyterians, Roman Catholics and Anglicans). In relating the message preached to its impact on people's lives, he found the three themes of "need for personal conversion", "duties of the Christian life" and "God's judgement" predominated in mainstream preaching (1995a, 84).

Ross found that subjective responses, emphasizing personal conversion or the duties of the Christian life, were generally given greater attention than teaching of core doctrines; preaching in the imperative was more common than the indicative (1995a, 84). Yet, twice as many Presbyterian sermons presented faith as acceptance of propositional statements than belief from the heart bringing assurance (1995a, 99). Sermons often focussed upon individual and personal change rather than social and communal dimensions

(1995a, 101). However, Presbyterians likewise envisaged their effect upon communities in terms of personal morality and conversion (1995a, 102). The impact of preaching upon Malawian national life was understood mostly in pre-Lausanne terms of passive cohesion of society and legitimization of the *status quo*, not challenging it with contemporary issues like human rights and justice. Ross summarized:

> Though the preaching is concerned mainly with the belief and behaviour of the individual, there is also a general expectation that it has a role to play in family life, community life and national life. (1995a, 103–104)

The overall impression is that preachers from protestant missionary denomination are still broadly influenced by the conversion priorities of their evangelical Western founders – the beliefs, behaviours and duties of the individual, and the stabilizing influence of such individuals upon their communities and wider society.

Ross found preachers from mainstream churches generally engaged poorly with African traditions like witchcraft and ancestors (1995a, 91). Only 8 out of 587 sermons sought responses in traditional African terms. Interviews suggested preachers were ambivalent about whether to perpetuate the original missionaries' disapproval of ancestors, or to adapt the message to accommodate traditional beliefs; many simply avoided such controversial subjects. Ambivalence toward ancestors and witchcraft was also evident among members; Christian faith and traditional religion seemed compartmentalized in the minds of believers from mainstream churches.

Furthermore, the intended message of preachers often did not coincide with what their audiences actually heard. For example, twice as many members as preachers thought the church had nothing to say on ancestors; likewise, 77 percent of Presbyterian preachers said, but only 59 percent of members heard them say that witchcraft was evil (1995a, 94). Though people were aware the church condemns witchcraft, many perceived their preachers not to take the issue seriously.

In the mainstream churches, 88 percent of the 587 sermons studied were said to be 'closely related' to the Bible reading. To this, Ross remarked:

> This underlines the massive importance of the Bible for mainstream Christianity in Africa. Not only are the texts being read week after week in parishes throughout the country but a serious effort is being made to expound them . . . Preaching,

by and large, attempts to explain, amplify, illustrate and apply a given passage of scripture. (1995a, 86)

Overall, Ross (1995a, 106) concluded that preaching in the mainstream churches was lively and influential; its message provided active debate on questions of faith, conduct, African culture and beliefs, yet retained tensions between the personal and the communal outworking of Christianity.

b)   *Popular Chichewa Preachers*

Wendland (2000) investigated the composition and rhetoric of popular Chichewa preachers from Malawi, focussing especially upon the revivalist preacher Shedrack Warne. Although Warne preached largely to Presbyterian audiences, he never received a formal theological education and knew little English. Hence, he may not have come under Western theological influences as much as mainstream preachers who had attended missionary denominational Bible schools.

Of particular interest are the theological and ethical subjects with which Warne and other revivalist preachers engaged. The revivalists encouraged spiritual renewal of the individual. They emphasized the spiritual powers of evil within a person, and how these may lead to sinful attitudes and behaviours. Their predominant approach towards faith was subjective (2000, 18), similar to the findings of Ross. However, revivalist preachers also presented the evil from a markedly African viewpoint in which Satan and his malevolent forces sought to act upon the community from outside. While Ross reported some ambivalence among mainstream Presbyterian preachers towards witchcraft, ancestors and magic, the Chichewa preachers positioned themselves closely alongside African belief systems in their contextualization (2000, 19).

In contrast to the three themes Ross noted, revivalist preachers placed "striking emphasis on practical, life-related subjects and felt needs" (2000, 23), notably bad behaviour (drunkenness, physical abuse, swearing), witchcraft (magic, cursing and sorcery, occult), and life after death (last things, heaven and hell). In the case of Warne, his preaching notably also had "doctrinal emphasis on the person and work of Christ" and "encouragement toward a Christian's personal testimony of the gospel" (2000, 23).

Both mainstream and revivalist preachers typically used several Scripture passages, but the two groups handled texts differently. While Ross reported "a serious effort is being made to expound" (1995a, 86–87) in mainstream preaching, Wendland concluded the revivalist preachers had "some significant omissions or deficiencies in the area of exegesis" (2000, 25). Revivalist preaching often lacked systematic explanation of text and/ or context of Bible passages. Popular preaching was strong on contextual exemplification, but weak on textual exposition (2000, 224), Scripture being used as a tool to illuminate the contemporary African situation.

c)   African Independent Churches

Chakanza wrote in 1981: "Independent churches clearly tend to formulate theology through the experience of human and religious needs whereas mainstream churches define human need from the viewpoint of their long tradition of theology" (in Mijoga 1996, 361). Mijoga investigated the factors influencing sermon preparation by AIC preachers: texts, themes, audience and occasion. From this 1989–90 study, he concluded their priority was to make preaching appear 'relevant'. Their hermeneutic principles were not formalized but practical, directed toward making the text understandable. AIC preachers generally sought God's guidance, chose texts and themes for the occasion and tried to match the preaching to the perceived needs, mood, education, and culture of the listeners. Mijoga summarized the approach as: "Everyone is free to start from anywhere and include what one considers to be important for the occasion or exegesis" (1996, 371). In this respect, preaching in the AICs would seem to mirror that of the popular preachers.

Mijoga commented on the potential dangers of such an interpretive approach (1996, 363). In the quest for relevance to contemporary Malawian life, it is possible that the occasion may drive the interpretation of the text. For example, a preacher may choose verses merely because they contain a particular key word (e.g. marriage), despite the passage actually referring to something else. Furthermore, the AICs are divided in their attitude toward theological training and use of Bible commentaries: some preachers valued such resources while others objected to their use as a matter of principle, asserting that only the Holy Spirit can call, guide and equip preachers – anything else is disobedience.

In 1996–1997, Mijoga (2000) sought to understand the methods used by AIC preachers to interpret the Bible. Whenever AIC preachers adopted a systematic verse-by-verse approach, the result was typically literal interpretation and simple retelling without characterisation or explanation of the text (2000, 43). Over half of all AIC sermons cited at least two Bible texts (2000, 18), yet most would have been proof texting, a common practice in both mainstream and AICs in Malawi. Mijoga said of the AICs: "the assumption here is that . . . we are dealing with nonliterate preachers and audiences, who preach and read the Bible uncritically" (2000, 14). He concluded it was unreasonable to expect them to use deductive text-based methodologies to perform systematic analysis of passages (2000, 13).

The AICs used a range of inductive channels of interpretation in their sermon preparation and delivery (prayers, songs, stories, proverbs, proof texts, rhetorical questions, exclamations and references to local situations) that were emotive, participatory and resembled African oral tradition (2000, 73–106). Such preaching expects real-time audience response, similarly to Warne and the popular preachers (Wendland 2000). Kalilombe (1999, 207–208) had observed previously that such methods were well suited for Biblical interpretation among nonliterate communities in Malawi.

Mijoga showed that in the preaching of AICs "the Bible is extensively used" (1996, 368), "is central in these churches . . . is looked at as an authority" (2000, 158) and suggested that the approach of mainstream churches and AICs to interpretation (thematic, verse-by-verse, storytelling), mood of delivery (imperative) and subjects tackled (theological: Christ, Holy Spirit, sin, law and end times; practical: Satan, illness, death, women, family) was similar (2000, 15). Mijoga therefore concluded "although the AICs are 'separate', they preach the same gospel as the mainstream churches" (2000, 15).

In summary, Mijoga's proposal that the AICs are authentic Malawian expressions of Christianity because they differ from mainstream churches primarily in their rituals of worship and celebration, not in their use of the Bible (2000, 193) seems broadly valid. However, it seems incorrect to conclude, "in terms of exposition there is no difference between the mainstream churches, popular preachers, and AICs" (2000, 18). It is naïve to overlook the differences that exist in Biblical interpretation:

1. Mainstream churches are more likely to have preachers with at least some training in critical methods due to education and church tradition. This is likely to offer greater exegetical control on the meaning(s) of the text.

2. Although Mijoga reasonably claims, "this Bible is important to all Christian churches in Malawi" (2000, 162), and preachers from all streams make "constant reference to the Bible" (2000, 28–29), nevertheless the manner of such use is surely more important than the number of texts quoted. With popular preachers and AICs,

texts merely "serve as the basis for a sermon" (2000, 18). The lack of exposition surely leaves them exegetically weak (2000, 17). Although strong on illustration, a question mark must remain over the driving force behind the topics being illustrated.

3. The AICs seek a hermeneutical conversation between the Bible text, the reader and contemporary African culture – even if they are not "vanguards of African culture" (Mijoga, 2000, 193). In contrast, the mainstream seems ambivalent toward engagement with issues like ancestors, polygamy, initiation rites and witchcraft. Since mainstream preaching bypasses African cultural issues and no interpretation is ever neutral, it will likely default towards Western paradigms which cannot easily relate to these issues.

1.7   Literary Context: Romans in Malawi

Narrative from both OT and NT is generally popular in Malawian preaching. What about nonnarrative? This section considers the use of Romans by mainstream, AIC and popular preachers based on the studies of Ross, Mijoga and Wendland.

Ross surveyed 259 mainstream Presbyterian services and found Romans (21 uses) was the most frequently quoted NT book after the four Gospels and Acts. It was used at least twice as often as any other NT book, and only Genesis and Isaiah from the OT were used more regularly than Romans (1995a, 87).

Mijoga surveyed 299 sermons in AICs, and found Romans (27 uses) was the most frequently used book after Matthew, Luke and John. It was read more often than Acts or any OT book, and at least twice as frequently as any other New Testament book (Mijoga 2000, 24). In the AICs, verses were cited throughout the letter (2000, 28),[2] and some verses were connected with themes for specific occasions or needs (Mijoga 1996, 369–370).[3]

Wendland analysed 100 sermons by popular preachers, and by contrast Romans was scarcely read whatsoever; the letter was never used as either a main text or minor citation by Shedrack Warne, and rarely quoted by others (Wendland 2000, 24–25). Instead, the popular preachers focussed on

---

2. Romans 1:14–15; 1:18–32; 1:23; 2:4; 3:23; 4:18–25; 5:12–21; 6:23; 8:1–6; 8:12–30; 8:14; 9:6–14; 10:1–4; 10:9; 11:33–36; 12:8; 12:9–10; 12:9–11; 12:11–12; 12:15; 13:11–14; 14:11; 15:4–13; 16:19.

3. faith – Rom 10:9; sin – Rom 3:25; apostleship – Rom 11:1–3, 13; baptism – Rom 6:3–4; death and affliction – Rom 8:9–17; ordination – Rom 12:1–2.

the narratives of the life of Christ in Matthew, Luke and John, to illuminate the contemporary African situation and felt needs. Perhaps these texts lend themselves more to their emotive style of preaching.

In summary, both mainstream and AIC preachers frequently quoted Romans, but rarely the popular preachers. It therefore has an existing base of use. From its content, Romans surely challenged its original first-horizon audience to consider both theological and practical questions, and could do likewise in the contemporary Malawian third-horizon. These factors make it an attractive candidate for studying the interpretation of a Pauline letter in provincial-rural Malawi.

1.8 Outline of Study

- Chapter 1 outlines the research questions and contexts of the study.

- Chapter 2 describes the field research methodology.

- Chapter 3 presents the results of field research: first, a summary profile of the Malawian church leaders questioned in this study; second, the socio-cultural/religious issues they experienced in their ministry.

- Chapter 4 presents a three-horizon contextual reading of Romans against the context of provincial-rural Malawi (modelled in chapter 3), and offers current use and further interpretation of the most popular verses/pairs.

- Chapter 5 further develops this Malawian reading of Romans with interpretation of paragraphs: five contextually important themes are interpreted against a background of socio-cultural and pastoral problems.

- Chapter 6 presents the conclusions of this study.

2

Research Methods

2.1   Introduction

Field research was conducted among 200 serving church leaders in provincial-rural Malawi. Data were collected in Central and Southern Malawi between 15 July – 8 August 2011 from pastors, elders, evangelists and women's leaders representing 33 different mainstream and AIC denominations.

This chapter outlines the research methods used: basic questionnaires, supplementary questionnaires and semi-structured interviews, augmented by observations from group discussions and contextual Bible studies.

2.2   Basic Questionnaires at Conferences

The basic questionnaire (appendix A) was distributed to each delegate at two church leaders' training conferences held in provincial-rural Malawi.[1] The questionnaire aimed to collect data to capture:

- a profile of each delegate as a church leader
- the key socio-cultural, religious and pastoral problems experienced in their ministries
- their recent use of Romans in preaching and/or teaching
- how they view Romans relating to Malawian life

The basic questionnaire comprised fourteen questions in English. It was distributed at the beginning of the conference for completion by the second

---

1. The Pastors' and Elders' Book Conferences both lasted three days and were organized by the Evangelical Bible College of Malawi in association with Zambesi Mission. See the report by Kanyumi (2011).

day. This overnight period gave opportunity to check information, reflect on answers and seek help with literacy. Malawian facilitators provided Chichewa-speaking support. Delegates could respond in Chichewa, and Chichewa-speaking assistants translated these into English. Data were transcribed into Excel spreadsheets and an Access database for analysis.

The basic questionnaire used straightforward English vocabulary to ask multiple choice and open-ended questions. Open-ended questions avoided priming respondents with limited, preselected answers. A draft was examined beforehand by three reviewers (British, Malawian and Zimbabwean) who commented on language clarity and its potential to elicit information for the research questions. Open responses were grouped around key words/concepts written in the delegates' answers. Nevertheless, such analysis of open responses is a second-horizon interpretative step that inevitably introduces some subjectivity from the analyst.

179 basic questionnaires were returned: 99 out of a possible 117 delegates at Liwonde, and 80 out of 97 at Mponela. This corresponds to 82–85 percent return rates at both locations, sufficiently high to consider the results to be representative of provincial-rural church leaders generally.

The first conference was held at Liwonde (population 30,000) in Southern Region.[2] Ethnically, this area is populated by the Yao people (largely Muslim) plus the Lomwe and some Ngoni and Chewa (Christian/ATR). The result is a mix of cultural and religious practices drawn from Folk Islam, Christianity and ATR. Most people in the town are familiar with English-speaking visitors, and some expatriates live there. At Liwonde, 74 percent of the questionnaires were completed in English rather than Chichewa.

The second conference was held at Mponela (population 14,000) in Central Region.[3] The predominant Chewa and Ngoni tribes widely practice ATR, frequently alongside elements of Christianity. Chewa traditional religion includes the Nyau 'Big Dance' *Gule wamkulu* (VanBreugel 2001, 125–168), an elaborate network of secret societies, initiations, rituals and cosmological beliefs. At Mponela, 64 percent of questionnaires were completed in English – slightly lower than Liwonde.

---

2. Liwonde is in Machinga district, 240 km southeast of Lilongwe. Liwonde serves as a regional centre and transportation hub with influence extending to the neighbouring districts of Balaka, Mangochi, and Zomba.
3. Mponela is in Dowa district, 60 km north of Lilongwe. Mponela has a predominantly agricultural economy and lacks tourism.

The basic questionnaire did not ask about the general education of delegates. This was introduced in subsequent profiling of 102 church leaders at a conference in Nsanje district of Southern Region. In Nsanje, only 52 percent of delegates had completed all eight years of primary school (Groves, unpublished). UN statistics indicate an average young Malawian has received only four years of primary education (UNDP Malawi, 2012), sufficient to give basic proficiency in Chichewa but not English. Pastors are often among the more educated in village communities. Church services and Bible readings in villages are exclusively in Chichewa (or local tribal languages), while most town services are in Chichewa, with a few offering an alternative English-speaking service for the few more-educated Malawians who prefer this.

2.3   Supplementary Questionnaires at Conferences

A supplementary questionnaire (appendix B) was distributed on day 2 to conference delegates who volunteered to complete it by day 3. The majority of questions were open ended, yielding qualitative answers. It explored in greater depth the socio-cultural and religious issues causing difficulties in their ministry, and sought insight into how Malawian Christians relate to Romans and might be given practical help to understand the text.

The two questionnaires were cross-referenced to create a single dataset for each delegate. Ideally, the supplementary questionnaire would have been completed by face-to-face interviews, but opportunity to discuss was limited by proficiency at conversational English, time within the conference programme, and the need of delegates to depart promptly at the end of each day. A few responses were collected by short (5–10 minute) interviews in English.

Of the 43 volunteers receiving and returning supplementary questionnaires, 20 were from Liwonde and 23 from Mponela. Additional information was therefore obtained from about a quarter of the 179 who returned basic questionnaires. Those willing to complete the supplementary questionnaire will inevitably have included the more educated church leaders. The qualitative interview responses were used to augment the numerical data of the questionnaires with additional descriptions and quotations.

2.4   Detailed Interviews with Senior Pastors

The supplementary questionnaire was used as a template for face-to-face interviews of 30 to 120 minute duration with four Malawian senior pastors.

Each came from a different church background: The first pastor (P1) was from a rural Pentecostal AIC south of Lilongwe. The second (P2) was from a mainstream Pentecostal church west of Lilongwe. The third (P3) was from a mainstream Malawian evangelical church in Blantyre, with experience working at a national level. The fourth (P4) was from a mainstream Malawian evangelical denomination in Blantyre, who was also a Bible college lecturer. These in-depth interviews provided detailed cultural and exegetical insight and contextual information.

2.5   Small Groups Discussions

Conference delegates were divided into groups of about ten people to discuss issues relating to ministry problems. Each group gave feedback to the plenary session in Chichewa, their reports translated into English and observations noted.

2.6   Contextual Bible Studies

Portions of Romans were discussed near Likuni by two groups of 6–8 untrained church deacons and wives using the Contextual Bible Study method (Riches 2010, 58–68). Observations were recorded.

2.7   Summary

The field research for this study uses multiple approaches (questionnaires, interviews, observations) to obtain quantitative and qualitative data from several Malawian sample populations:

- A main dataset of 179 conference delegates from two provincial-rural areas of Malawi.

- A subset of 43 delegate volunteers providing supplementary information.

- Four senior pastors who gave in-depth interviews.

- Group discussions by conference delegates.

- Two Contextual Bible Study groups.

3

Modelling the Third-Horizon

3.1 Introduction

This chapter describes the results of field research into the socio-cultural context of Christian ministry in provincial-rural Malawi. First, it characterises the church leaders of provincial-rural Malawi by profiling (section 3.2). Second, it outlines the socio-cultural and pastoral problems they face in their ministry (section 3.3).

3.2 Profile of Church Leaders

This section presents the results of field research to create a detailed profile of the 179 delegates at the Liwonde and Mponela training conferences that completed the basic questionnaire. It is assumed that this model is an accurate reflection of the wider population of pastors and lay workers in provincial-rural Malawi who exercise Bible teaching ministries and are willing to attend conference training.

Five characteristics of the delegates were modelled in the profile:

    a) Church Role and Length of Service

    b) Gender

    c) Location and Size of Churches

    d) Denomination

    e) Previous Training for Ministry

The profile is assumed to reflect the wider population of pastors and lay workers in provincial-rural Malawi. It only includes field data from serving church leaders who were able and willing to attend the conference and volunteer information about their ministry. The results will therefore reflect the situation of rural church leaders in Malawi who hold a positive outlook on such ministry training and Biblical instruction. However, it may be at odds with the views of pastors (mostly from certain AICs) who argue that they must rely solely upon the Holy Spirit for knowledge and inspiration; such church leaders are indeed unlikely to have been willing to attend the training conference where the data was collected.

a)   Church Role and Length of Service

In total, 179 delegates completed questionnaires (table 1). Of these, 105 described themselves as 'pastor' (59 percent) and 74 as 'non-pastor' (41 percent). From discussions, it was clear that the non-pastors group served in a range of local church leadership roles including lay elder, prayer house leader, evangelist, youth leader, women's worker and pastor's wife. In Liwonde, the pastors group comprised 50 people, which was 51 percent of all delegates. In Mponela, there were 55 pastors, which corresponded to 69 percent of the delegates. The Liwonde delegates contained 49 non-pastors, and Mponela contained 25 non-pastors.

At both locations, the pastors ranged in ministry experience from those recently called to those with over a decade in service (table 1). Almost a quarter of them were in their first two years, and over half in the first five years of ministry. Once called, the majority of pastors would remain in service until death, undertaking other employment alongside, if necessary.[1] Hence, the number with a relatively short service history may reflect the large number of new churches and pastors in rural Malawi, and their recognition of need for training.

For cross-tabulation analysis, the 'pastors' were considered in two roughly equal-sized groups – an 'inexperienced pastor' group with 0–5 years in ministry (55 delegates), and an 'experienced pastor' group that had served for 6 or more years (50 delegates).

b)   Gender

The gender distribution of the delegates was 79 percent male and 14 percent female (and 7 percent unspecified). The proportion of female delegates was

---

1. Interview Pastor P2

slightly higher in Liwonde (17 percent) than Mponela (10 percent), due to a greater number of the non-pastors being women at Liwonde (29 percent) than Mponela (12 percent). As might be expected in Malawi, the majority of pastors were male (84 percent) at both locations. The minority of female pastors (8 percent) were mostly from AICs. It was a goal of the conference organisers that female as well as male church leaders would enrol as delegates, to help support the Bible ministry of women-to-women.

c)   Location and Size of Churches

Liwonde and Mponela are provincial market towns with well-populated rural hinterlands. In rural Malawi, villages are characterised by lack of electricity or a marketplace where people can gather. Frequently piped water is not available, but only a well or river, and many residents receive little or no primary schooling.[2] In contrast, such amenities are normally available in provincial towns. Trading centres (Malawi–Project, 2012), typically comprising a few small shops, a bar/beer hall and a part-time bank are increasingly arising in village areas. These function as a bridge to town life for villagers living beyond walking distance from a market. Rural people frequently gather there, offering an attractive opportunity for a church-planting initiative. In villages, prostitution, witchcraft and traditional medicine may occur openly.[3]

At Liwonde, the conferences delegates came equally from churches in town (50 percent) and village locations (44 percent), with a minority based at trading centres (5 percent). In contrast, at Mponela the majority of delegates were drawn from a village (59 percent), with the remainder from the town (26 percent) and trading centres (15 percent). A higher proportion of delegates at Mponela thus had ministries based in villages or trading centres than in Liwonde.

Table 2 shows the size range of the churches within which delegates served. The most frequent congregational size range was 25–100 people, these churches being associated with 45 percent of all church leaders. This was the most common size of congregation to be served by both pastors and non-pastors, and at both Liwonde and Mponela (data not shown). Smaller churches or prayer houses comprising 0–25 people were led by 16 percent of delegates, while larger congregations of 100–250 people or of 250+ people

---

2. Interview Pastor P2
3. Interview Pastor P1

were served by 18 percent and 21 percent of delegates respectively. The picture is therefore one of congregational diversity, but with a majority of delegates ministering in churches of less than 100 people.

Cross-tabulation of church location against the size of its congregation (table 3) shows that the majority of leaders of small (0–25 people) and medium-sized (25–100) congregations were village-based. Indeed, two-fifths of all pastors (41 percent) were in village congregations of less than 100 people. In contrast, the majority of those leading large (100–250) and especially the very large (250+) congregations were based in towns. A quarter of all pastors (23 percent) were in town congregations of greater than 100 people.

Cross-tabulation of the length of service of church leaders against their church's location (table 4) demonstrated that a majority of pastors with less than 10 years' experience serve in village congregations. In the case of the newly appointed pastors (0–2 years) about three-quarters are village-based. However, the majority of the most experienced pastors (10+ years) are located in town churches. The same patterns are broadly observed in both Liwonde and Mponela, though the sample number of delegates in each category becomes too small to analyse all three criteria together.

Interviewing revealed that many denominations would expect new pastors initially to serve near their homes, based on the principle of "beginning in Jerusalem" (Acts 1:8) and then moving outwards.[4] Pragmatically, this allows new pastors to continue subsistence farming or other business activities to help support themselves. Yet other denominations follow a tradition of centrally appointing a new pastor where there is no leadership, though again this is likely to be a poor rural congregation. Once pastors have established their ministry, they may get opportunity to move elsewhere, including the larger town churches. Since the large town churches were the ones best able to send more than one delegate to the conference, the correlation between small congregational size, village location and inexperienced pastors could be even stronger than the numbers suggest.

d)   Denominations

The two conferences attracted delegates from a total of 33 different denominations (table 5). At Liwonde, there were 23 different denominations present, 12 being missionary-instituted and 11 AICs. These were drawn from

---

4. Interview Pastor P2

11 Pentecostal and 12 non-Pentecostal denominations. At Mponela, there were 19 different denominations present, 9 being missionary-initiated and 10 AICs, 12 were Pentecostal denominations but only 7 were non-Pentecostal.

Of the 99 delegates at Liwonde, a small majority were from non-Pentecostal (57 people) versus Pentecostal denominations. Likewise, a small majority were from missionary-initiated (65 people) rather than African-independent churches. The most commonly represented denominations at Liwonde were the Church of Central Africa Presbyterian (20 delegates), Assemblies of God (12), Good News Revival Church (8), Zambezi Evangelical Church (8), Evangelical Baptist (7) and the Living Waters Church (5).

Of the 80 delegates at Mponela, a large majority were from Pentecostal denominations (60 people). However, just a small majority were from missionary-initiated denominations (48 people) rather than the AICs. The most commonly represented denominations at Mponela were Assemblies of God (32 people) and Living Waters Church (16), followed by New Last Truth of God (6 people), Church of Central Africa Presbyterian (4) and African Abraham Church International (3). A main difference from Liwonde is that just two denominations together account for 60 percent of Mponela delegates. Overall, both conferences included a balanced mix of the different Malawian protestant church traditions active in the vicinity – evangelical and Pentecostal.

e)   Previous Training for Ministry

Almost three quarters of those in the pastors group (70 percent) claimed to have completed either an extension course or period of full-time study at a Bible school; in this study, these people are considered to be 'trained'. The remaining pastors (30 percent) had received no formal instruction, or only participated in a short course; for this study, they are classified as 'untrained'.

For the non-pastors group, only about a quarter were trained (26 percent) and three-quarters were untrained (74 percent). While a majority of lay church leaders in the UK are likely also to lack formal training, the higher level of general education in the West and greater availability of Bibles and study material distinguishes the two situations.

Combining the pastor and non-pastor groups, 52 percent of all conference delegates were trained according to these criteria. This indicates that almost half of church leaders serve in their churches without basic Bible school training. Since the conferences at which this research was conducted will attract as delegates those church leaders who are practically able and theologically willing to participate in locally delivered, low-cost training, we may conclude that the proportion of trained leaders in the wider church is likely to be rather lower.

Furthermore, many of those delegates classified as trained will not have received seminary or Bible college level training leading to formal theological courses at Certificate or Diploma level (Ross, 1995b). It is popularly quoted that 90–95 percent of Malawian church leaders lack any formal seminary training (Ijalasi, 2012; SIM, 2012). First, entry to such courses in Malawi generally requires completion of a full four years of secondary education. This prerequisite is impossible for most people in rural areas of Malawi due to poverty (secondary schooling is not free of charge in Malawi), social and economic pressures (families may require them to work, and/or not value education, especially in the case of girls), and geographical inaccessibility (there are very few secondary schools situated in rural areas). Furthermore, the costs of seminary courses are themselves prohibitive, except for a minority of students who may receive externally funded bursaries from denominations or missions.

When the denominational affiliation of delegates was cross-tabulated against level of training, the mainstream missionary denominations had a slightly higher proportion of trained leaders than the AICs. This pattern was observed with both the trained pastors (mainstream 77 percent, AICs 61 percent) and non-pastors (mainstream 29 percent, AICs 18 percent).

The existence of a dedicated denominational Bible training school[5] was cross-tabulated against existing level of training for each delegate. This comparison revealed that of the 65 pastors that came from a denomination with its own Bible school, 75 percent were trained, while of the 40 pastors from a denomination lacking its own Bible school, only 38 percent were trained. For the 57 non-pastors from a denomination with a Bible school, only 28 percent were trained, while of the 17 non-pastors from a denomination without a Bible school, a mere 18 percent were trained. From this, we conclude that the existence of a denomination Bible school greatly increases the likelihood that a pastor will have been trained. To a lesser degree this was the case with non-pastors, though their level of training was always low.

While training is most strongly associated with being a pastor, in the light of the rapid growth rate of the Malawian church, particularly the

---

5. Interview Pastor P2

AICs, extensive lay participation in congregational leadership and church planting is necessary and to be welcomed. However, the low levels of Biblical, theological and practical training for ministry, especially for non-pastors in all denominations of the Malawian church, could pose a significant challenge to the critical interpretation and application of Scripture in Malawi.

Summary of the Profile

59 percent of church leaders were pastors and 41 percent non-pastors. The non-pastor group included elders, prayer-house leaders, evangelists, youth leaders, women's workers and pastor's wives. Pastors divided equally between those with less than five years in ministry and those with more than five years' experience. About one-tenth of the pastors were female, mostly from AICs.

Provincial-rural churches were based either in towns, villages or trading centres. Slightly more Liwonde leaders were in the town than in villages, but a clear majority of Mponela leaders were village based. This reflects the relative size of the two towns. In both locations, congregations varied in size from prayer houses (0–25 people) to large town churches (250+ people); the most common was 25–100 people. Smaller congregations (0–100 people) tended to be in villages, while larger congregations were generally town based. The most experienced pastors tended to serve in larger town-based congregations, while inexperienced church pastors served in small village churches/prayer houses. Most new pastors serve at first in villages before moving into a town as their ministry develops.

Church leaders came from 33 denominations, equally divided between missionary-instituted and AICs, Pentecostals and non-Pentecostals. The views expressed by church leaders in this work will reflect this range of Malawian protestant church traditions. Half of church leaders had received some training, concentrated in 70 percent of pastors but only 26 percent of non-pastors. Mainstream denominations and those having their own Bible school had higher proportions of trained leaders.

3.3   Socio-Cultural and Pastoral Issues

This section outlines the spectrum of issues that the provincial-rural church leaders raised as important within their congregations. When delegates were asked to describe which aspects of Malawian life and culture were causing difficulties,[6] 231 issue-instances were highlighted collectively by 105 delegates in Liwonde, and 169 issues by 74 delegates in Mponela.

Problems were organised into one of four major groups (table 6) for discussion below. These were: (a) Muslim Culture/Practices; (b) African Traditional Culture/Practices; (c) Sexual Ethics and Marriage Problems; (d) Other Attitudes/Behaviours and Poverty. These are not mutually exclusive groupings and several issues could have been categorised otherwise.[7]

a)   *Muslim Culture and Practices*

Liwonde is a major centre for the predominantly Muslim (80–95 percent) Yao tribe. Dicks says, "Islam is the structural religion with which [the Yao] most identify, with traditional religion playing a dominant yet more underlying role, which for many Yao people means it still pervades every aspect of life" (2012, 98). In practice, issues caused by Muslim and/or ATR practices are likely to result from a blend of both religions.

Difficulties were reported because there was "fusion of Islamic lifestyle into [church] culture",[8] either though passive infiltration or active transfer. Such Muslim practices were deeply embedded in Liwonde churches (15 percent of Liwonde issues), but only peripheral in Dowa District (<2 percent of Mponela issues) where Muslims comprise a small minority.

How did church leaders experience these difficulties? First, Christian families were encouraged to embrace Muslim circumcision as a social transition rite for their 10–15 year old boys (Dicks 2012, 124–152). Peer pressure was exerted on the children themselves.[9] Not to circumcise even caused segregation *within* churches.[10]

Second, church members were offered incentives to adopt Muslim practices, for example:

- Yao initiation ceremonies . . . and Muslim almsgiving [create difficulties], especially during their month of Ramadan through

---

6. Question 7 of the basic questionnaire and Question 1 of the advanced questionnaire: '*What aspects of Malawian life and culture cause difficulties in your church?*'

7. Anonymous footnote quotations from Liwonde or Mponela (Dowa) delegates are referenced in the format (Delegate Lnn) or (Delegate Dnn), where nn is the delegate conference registration number.

8. Delegate L94 (Assemblies of God; village)

9. Delegate L58 (Church of Central Africa, Presbyterian; town)

10.   Delegate L39 (Zambezi Evangelical Church; village)

distribution of slaughtered goats to everybody. Some of our members flock to them, causing problems in our church.[11]

Third, delegates described the difficulty of outreach to Muslims and problems integrating converts into the church. For example:

- I am serving in Muslims area where they believe that by just wash[ing] hands and face you become holy before the Lord. To me it is a big hindrance. It takes time for them to understand the word 'repent'.[12]

- Most Christians who were once Muslims believe in polygamy type of life, so that spirit is still in these newly converted Christians. Then they find it difficult to leave that culture.[13]

In summary, Christian discipleship in Liwonde is hindered by the import of Islamic ritual practices into church life, and failure culturally to integrate Muslim converts, who remain isolated.

b)   African Traditional Culture and Practices

Liwonde and Mponela were both heavily influenced by magic, witchcraft, diviners and traditional medicine (50 percent of Liwonde issues, 56 percent of Mponela issues). One pastor described witchcraft as 'rampant' in his area.[14] Of particular concern was the impact of traditional culture and religion on people *within* churches. Most declared witchcraft to be incompatible with Christian faith, contrary to the Bible, and a source of spiritual backsliding (i.e. against the message of the missionaries):

- Witchcraft is still a problem affecting members of the church. They profess to be church members but are secretly serving other gods.[15]

- People believe in witchcraft and sorcery, so those that are not deep rooted in faith may sometimes revert back to old ways of life when in trouble.[16]

---

11.   Delegate L202 (Zambezi Evangelical Church; trading-centre)
12.   Delegate L36 (Assemblies of God; trading-centre)
13.   Delegate D39 (Church of Central Africa, Presbyterian; village)
14.   Delegate D55 (Church of Central Africa, Presbyterian; town)
15.   Delegate D58 (Church of Central Africa, Presbyterian; village)
16.   Delegate L73 (Church of Central Africa, Presbyterian; town)

The attraction and dangers of diviners and traditional medicine men (whom the interviewees call 'witchdoctors') were highlighted:

- For a long time there were no hospitals. People used roots and leaves to cure diseases. If sick, they go to the herbalist who says you must face one way then the other. He is making a demonic ritual . . . When herbal medicine passes through a witchdoctor, the Devil wants to change your way of thinking. That is a big problem in a church.[17]

Detailed interviews revealed examples of failure, guilt and apostasy due to ATR:

- People see Christianity not offering the salvation they are looking for. For example, they are looking for healing but do not find it, so they go to witchdoctors. If they have no children and have prayed for them, then they go to the witchdoctor for 'blood medicine'. If robbed in their house and the church does not help, they go to the witchdoctor who does magic. Then they become shy to come back to church, especially if the witchdoctor's 'salvation' seems to have worked.[18]

They expressed the need for Bible teaching in rural areas to encourage discipleship and prevent apostasy:

- Some people confess to be Christians, but have no deep roots. Whenever something happens to them, they find it hard to rely on God. They meet traditional healers to seek help. In urban areas this is not happening much, but it is a big issue in rural areas where Biblical truth is not taught.[19]

African tradition views life as a continuum stretching from before birth to after death, initiation ceremonies marking the major social transitions (Dicks 2012, 124). Malawian Christians often continue practising transition rituals[20] at birth (VanBreugal 2001, 178–185; Dicks 2012, 152–154), puberty (VanBreugal 2001, 185–198) or death-burial (VanBreugal 2001, 97–123):

---

17.   Interview Pastor P1
18.   Interview Pastor P2
19.   Interview Pastor P3
20.   Delegate L32 (Roman Catholic Church; village)

- Rituals to new born baby to protect them from unexpected problems and during funerals to protect the ones alive and make easy burial of the deceased.[21]

Chinamwali marks the social transition of teenage girls from childhood to maturity. Girls are instructed through songs, dancing and drama about good citizenship, sexual behaviour, marriage and childbearing. Recognising its key role in community life, there have been genuine attempts to Christianize this rite (Longwe, 2007; Fiedler, 2007).

As with circumcision, the Muslim *sadaka* ancestor ceremony engages whole communities and confuses Christian worship.[22] *Sadaka* includes readings from the Koran and eating a remembrance meal (Dicks 2012, 101):

- Most Christians conduct *sadaka* at harvest time, saying their ancestral spirits want the food.[23]

The Nyau mask cult *Gule Wamkulu* (VanBreugal 2001, 125–168) poses a significant challenge to the church in Mponela. This Chewa secret society reveres ancestors and brings a symbolic representation of the spirit world into special occasions like funerals and *chinamwali*. *Gule* dancers hide anonymously behind masks and inside wild animal costumes, demanding to be viewed as the empowered spirits of the dead, now reunited with the living. They often act with impunity and so are associated with fear, ritual dread and extortion of money. Traditional Chewa funerals are major community occasions, and everyone in the village is expected to participate. An AIC pastor said of this:

- People are practising something demonic at the feast; they see it as offering money to demons, not God . . . They say you must pay a cow so you can bury your dead in the graveyard, or no one will come to your own funeral. This puts pressure on Christians . . . As the Pastor, I tell them to identify themselves as Christians ahead of time to the Chief and Village Headman. They know a person is then not touchable by traditional beliefs. They know you will not do the Nyau dances or allow your children to do so . . . In most

---

21.   Delegate L62 (Zambezi Evangelical Church; town)
22.   *Sadaka* is derived from an Arabic word *sadaqa* via Swahili Islam, meaning remembrance.
23.   Delegate L39 (Zambezi Evangelical Church; village)

villages, they let the Christians pass by if they are open about their faith.[24]

Puberty transitions often take place while *Gule* dancers perform at funerals.[25] Boys aged 8–18 are forced to initiate without easy escape afterwards.[26]

- They force you to be initiated. You go back home wanting to be Godly. You have to tell your fellow Christians you have been forced, and the pastor finds you are demon possessed. It's like a rape.[27]

Gule Wamkulu encompasses a range of Chewa traditions which impact negatively upon Christian belief and practice:

- Nyau teaches that participants should not believe in Jesus Christ.[28]

- In our church, most of the people have life style of *Gule wamkulu* that makes them hostile and rude to church rules.[29]

Gule Wamkulu is viewed as incompatible with Christ's role as mediator and his message of love and hope. A contemporary attempt to inculturate Nyau into Christianity (Aguilar 2009, 105) by comparing ancestral spirits with Christian 'saints' seems theologically and practically naïve.

In summary, traditional African culture and practices are endemic in provincial-rural Malawi, despite the prevalence of Christianity in many areas. Witchcraft, traditional medicine and transition ceremonies are especially visible in the villages. Church leaders must offer Biblical teaching and pastoral support to prevent regression when people encounter difficulties in their lives.

c)   *Sexual Ethics and Marital Problems*

Traditional African sexual and marriage practices created problems (14 percent of Liwonde issues; 21 percent of Mponela issues). Male polygamy (a man having more than one wife) is in the culture of both ATR and folk Islam, and accounted for over half of all the relationship issues. Some in the church claim justification from OT examples:

---

24.   Interview Pastor P1
25.   Interview Pastor P2
26.   Delegate L87 (Living Waters Church; town)
27.   Interview Pastor P1
28.   Delegate D39 (Church of Central Africa, Presbyterian; village)
29.   Delegate D42 (Assemblies of God; village)

- People are saying that they are doing this [polygamy] because other strong men of God did this like Abraham, Jacob, Solomon and others.[30]

Interviews illustrated the deep practical problems polygamy gives to pastors:

- A person may be converted, but have three wives. If you take him into the church then other people think polygamy is OK. If you don't take him, they think salvation depends upon behaviour not faith. If you say to get rid of the extra wives, you create a pastoral problem; you are saying Christ comes to destroy families.[31]

Polygamy spawns other sins, like lying and hatred:

- Many believers in Christianity tend to pretend having one wife yet they have other women around them.[32]

- [Polygamy] encourages hatred among the women married to one man.[33]

Marital breakdown and divorce were also caused by oppressive and violent male behaviour and infidelity.

- In families, husbands are believed to be the only ones to make decisions for their families. This often makes men cruel and violent to their wives, leading to marriage breakdown.[34]

- The idea that men are superior to women is inside the church and brings fighting within the family. The man thinks he can sleep around because he is superior, but he divorces the woman if she does this.[35]

Women feel oppressed and powerless to control their bodies before, during or after marriage:

- Traditional culture says it is sin for a lady to reject to assist men that need sexual actions.[36]

---

30. Delegate D75 (Assemblies of God; trading-centre)
31. Interview Pastor P2
32. Delegate L32 (Roman Catholic; village)
33. Delegate D39 (Church of Central Africa, Presbyterian; village)
34. Delegate L73 (Church of Central Africa, Presbyterian; town)
35. Interview Pastor P2
36. Delegate D36 (Assemblies of God; town)

- Women are oppressed and because of culture they remain quiet. They do not believe that God can change their situation.[37]

- The *Kulowa kufa* practice of sexual cleansing, a widow having to sleep with a *fisi* meaning the late husband's brother or someone else designated for this.[38]

Although the Yao (Dicks 2012, 122) and most Chewa (Sear 2008, 279) are matrilineal societies, pastors sometimes needed to help widows gain their human rights and free themselves from controlling male relatives.[39]

Prostitution occurred in a few churches.[40] Boys were encouraged in premarital sex to demonstrate adulthood. These actions were identified as contrary to Christian ethics.[41]

In summary, infidelity and oppression by men are a major cause of considerable suffering and resentment by Malawian women, for which contextual Biblical teaching is required.

d)   Other Attitudes and Behaviours and Poverty

A range of problematic attitudes and behaviours were reported in rural churches (14 percent of Liwonde issues; 17 percent of Mponela issues). Foremost was male beer-drinking culture and drunkenness. This is culturally associated with 'true membership' of certain tribes.[42] In response, most churches require members to abstain completely from beer.[43]

Apathy, nonparticipation, overreliance on leaders, gossiping, lying, boasting, lack of love, intolerance, disunity, ethnic divisions, inappropriate dress, disputing and unruly behaviour were all reported. A female pastor reported:

- People live a gossiping life. [They] decide not to come to attend the activities of the church instead they gather together from sunrise until sunset speaking about others, then later come to tell you "Pastor, I was busy, that is why I didn't come for church

---

37.   Delegate D9 (Charismatic Redeemed Ministries International, female pastor; town)
38.   Delegate L70 (Kingdom Gospel Church; town)
39.   Interview Pastor P1
40.   Delegate D35 (Assemblies of God; trading-centre)
41.   Delegate L87 (Living Waters Church; town)
42.   Delegate D20 (Victory Assemblies of God; village)
43.   Interview Pastor P2

work". They are lying and bring difficulties because it makes the church work to stop.[44]

Church leaders were themselves sometimes the cause of problems: money, power or popularity may be sought for selfish reasons, and so failing to preach and serve.

- Unbelievers in congregation are power hungry to be in positions of authority. This is a particular problem for new converts trying to move too fast.[45]

- Because of poverty and love of money, many people go for ministry, not because they have been called but because they want to feed their stomach.[46]

In summary, the provincial-rural church faces many problems that arise from ungodly attitudes and behaviour. Some of these are culturally induced, while others result from sin and selfishness that is driven by insecurity, pride, poverty and fear.

3.4   Discussion

People in provincial towns are likely to differ from those in rural villages in terms of work, education, mobility and wealth.[47] These differences may affect their reading of Scripture and the cultural presuppositions they bring to it.
Provincial town churches might include:

- a few professionals, e.g. engineers, teachers, managers or administrators

- shop/market traders, skilled craft workers

- manual labourers

- migrant workers, increasing tribal diversity

- unemployed/beggars, struggling to survive

- women, working alongside men outside of the home

---

44.   Delegate D84 (Living Waters Church, female pastor; village)
45.   Delegate L38 (Church of Christ; village)
46.   Delegate D24 (Assemblies of God; trading-centre)
47.   Interview Pastor P2

Village populations, in comparison, are more stable and largely mono-ethnic; their churches might include:

- small-scale subsistence farmers growing crops and/or keeping livestock
- manual labourers doing piecework, e.g. brick moulding or trench digging
- landless families, reliant on others for shelter and protection
- magicians and traditional healers
- women, rarely working away from their farms

This chapter presents a model for the third-horizon context of provincial-rural Malawi. The picture is one of a largely under-trained Malawian church leadership set against a catalogue of socio-cultural and pastoral problems.

Lack of training was most acutely expressed among non-pastors in the AICs. Lay leadership is vital to support the rapid growth of the Malawian church. However, the low levels of training for ministry, could pose a significant challenge to the interpretation and application of Scripture to Malawian life. Many non-pastors did not appear even to own a Bible.

Larger town churches may have planted prayer houses in villages or trading centres as a result of evangelistic campaigns. Manglos (2010, 426) noted for a mainstream Pentecostal denomination that "the single pastor ultimately directs and shapes the messages of the church, and is mostly free from denominational oversight". Interviewing suggested that senior pastors may informally take responsibility as bishops/overseers for novice pastors and lay leaders. Helping experienced church leaders to train others may therefore be the key to making an impact across an area.

Church leaders encounter a wide range of challenging socio-cultural and pastoral problems, especially in the villages where ATR is freely expressed and traditional cultures like Nyau are difficult to displace.[48] Leaders of churches are among the better educated in the villages, often facing additional community responsibilities like problem solving in social, sexual and political spheres (Manglos 2011, 334). However, profiling indicates that village-based pastors typically have the least experience of ministry, and many lack training. The situation is hardest for the non-pastors doing pastoral roles, three-quarters of whom are untrained.

---

48.   Interview Pastor P2

African cultures like polygamy, witchcraft and traditional medicine are especially visible in villages. Many moral, sexual and behavioural problems also have roots in traditional culture. Cultures may blend, for example, Yao folk Islam and ATR in Liwonde. Parallel practices may arise in diverse cultural traditions, e.g. circumcision in both Muslim (Yao) and Nyau (Chewa) contexts. Formulating a contextual yet Biblical response is most challenging for untrained, inexperienced church leaders.

Christian 'born again' conversion may be viewed in rural Malawi "as a change in moral practice rather than a change in religious beliefs" (Manglos 2010, 411), and not as "an individual coming to faith" (2010, 427). This correlates with the previously noted emphasis of some Malawian preachers on "duties of the Christian life" (Ross 1995a, 84) and "practical, life-related subjects and felt needs" (Wendland 2000, 23). It seems that most problems faced by church leaders are pragmatic and grounded in culture. Manglos affirms young Malawians face a decision "whether, given their material constraints, they are able or willing to follow the moral prescriptions of a society infused with a mixture of monotheistic religion, African spirituality, and the influence of the modern lifestyle choices" (Manglos 2010, 427). Christian 'born again' conversion by this reckoning is experiential not cerebral.

Chapters 4 and 5 will consider how church leaders use Romans, and how it might be interpreted contextually for pastoral benefit in the socio-cultural milieu of rural Malawi defined by this model of the third horizon.

4

From Rome to Malawi

4.1 Introduction

In chapter 3, a profile was compiled of a largely under-trained Malawian church leadership facing a range of socio-cultural and pastoral problems in their ministry. In chapters 4 and 5, this perspective is adopted as a model representation of contemporary provincial-rural Malawi in the third-horizon. It is then used within a three-horizon study to develop possible contextual interpretations of Romans.

This chapter first considers aspects of the original first-horizon context: why Paul wrote Romans and the likely identity of his original recipients. In doing so, it draws parallels between the possible first- and natural third-horizon audiences (section 4.2).

Second, using field research, this chapter investigates existing interpretations of Romans in provincial-rural Malawi, and suggests potential new ones:

i) By confirming the extent that preachers in Liwonde and Mponela use Romans, and the factors influencing its use (section 4.3).

ii) By identifying through field research, those verses of Romans that are most used in preaching and the subjects they are used to speak about (section 4.4 a-d, part i "Existing Use").

iii) By performing exegetical analysis in the first-horizon and interacting this with the model third-horizon context, to imagine how Romans might be read through rural Malawian eyes (section 4.4 a-d, part ii "Between Horizons").

The provisional meaning 'behind the text' is used to constrain the range of African reader responses acceptable 'in front of the text'. In performing interpretation, OT understandings of δικαιοσύνη ('righteousness/justice') emerge as a particular focus of discussion in this chapter.

4.2   Between Three Horizons

The Letter to the Romans is difficult to understand in any culture. A Malawian senior pastor remarked:

- Romans is not widely used [in Malawi], I think because Paul's theology in his letters and especially in Romans is not simple. It is particularly difficult for those with poor educational background who have not studied the Word of God properly. Many churches are led by untrained lay people who find [Romans] hard to teach to their congregations.[1]

Due to its pivotal role in the history of the Western church (Augustine, Luther etc.), it is easy to view Romans as a "compendium of Christian doctrine" (Melanchthon), a timeless theological treatise for intellectuals to discuss in exclusive Roman academies. But the letter is also an occasional document, written to real people experiencing concrete life situations (Donfried 1991, 103–104; Esler 2003, 9; Moo 1991, 10–13). While theology is implied, it is "task theology" (Fee 2003, 58).

In this section, we will consider the socio-historical context of the letter: why and to whom it was written. Starting from a second-horizon, it will try to reconstruct some aspects of the ancient first-horizon in the light of current scholarship. The chapter will then attempt to interface this first-horizon with the Malawian third-horizon.

a)   First-Horizon: Ancient Rome

The general consensus is that the letter was written by Paul (1:1)[2] in 56–58 CE, to the Roman church which he had never visited.[3] Paul paints a picture of congregational diversity: Hellenistic-Jewish and God-fearing Gentile

---

1. Interview Pastor P3
2. All unattributed chapter and verse references in this format refer to the Letter to the Romans.
3. 1:7–13; 15:23

believers, male and female, diverse social standing, many originating outside Rome (1:14–16; 3:29–30; 16:3–16; Witherington 2004, 10). The Gentile majority were the likely intended recipients (Dunn 1988a, xlv; Moo 1991, 13), but occasionally discoursing with a Jewish interlocutor. Witherington summarizes: "Paul . . . is primarily addressing Gentile Christians in Rome, although he is happy for Jewish Christians to overhear this conversation" (2004, 8). Paul's use of Jewish-style question-answer diatribe (whether with a real or imagined interlocutor), and numerous references to the LXX suggests the recipients appreciated OT traditions.

The reasons for Paul writing Romans have been debated extensively (Morris 1988, 7–20; Moo 1991, 16–22). Although the letter is not explicit about its occasion and purpose, Paul reveals the identity, ethnicity and social status of those in the church through the 'frame' of the letter in 1:1–15 and 15:14–16:27 (Esler 2003, 109–134).[4] Paul's motivation may be summarized as: "apologetic" against misunderstanding his gospel; "missionary" to secure his sending base; and/or "pastoral" to counteract divisions (Dunn 1988a, liv–lviii).

What were relationships like between Jewish and Gentile Christians? Perhaps the house-church organisation and lack of apostolic foundation meant authority was fragmentary in Rome (Witherington 2004, 9), needing apologetic teaching and/or pastoral intervention. The expulsion of the Jews from Rome in 49 CE may have triggered social and cultural division and caused leadership increasingly to pass to Gentiles. Although without serious rifts (as in Galatia), the establishment of scattered house churches (16:5) and subsequent return and re-integration of Jewish returnees in 54–55 CE may have strengthened 'intragroup' identities (Esler 2003, 27–29), so exacerbating social tensions, factions and distance between parties (Donfried 1991, 102–103; Schreiner 1998, 13–21); Romans has been read in the context of such Jew-Gentile tensions (Das 2007, 201–202).

Paul's stated plan was to take the gospel west to Spain (15:22–24), before which he may have wanted to secure his Roman support base and apostolic authority (Esler 2003, 115–116; reviewed Schreiner 1998, 22–23). His affirmation that every ethnic group stands equally under sin and grace may have been written with this missionary motivation; Romans has been read in relation to this mission (Jewett 2007, 58–59, 87–91).

---

4. This argument assumes chapter 16 to be original part of the letter (Esler 2003, 116).

Who did Paul write to? It is generally understood that the Roman church comprised a number of house-church congregations (16:3–16; Esler 2003, 120–122). Where did these meet and who comprised their membership? Oakes (2009) has recently combined archaeology from ancient Pompeii and the Biblical text to reconstruct a representative model of a Roman house church. He argues that these were not hosted by elite patrons, but met in relatively modest rooms or commercial workshops (perhaps 45m² area) in poor, low-lying areas, perhaps tenements, and were patronless and egalitarian (2009, 89–97). Their membership was estimated hypothetically to be about 30 men and women from four social categories:

1) skilled craft worker, e.g. cabinet maker, (host)

2) near-destitute unskilled craft worker, e.g. stone worker (freed slave)

3) low-status slave, e.g. boiler stoker

4) sexually-exploited slave, e.g. barmaid

Oakes shows how major themes of Romans, like salvation, justification and adoption, might have been perceived by this group, and how the ethical implications of Romans might have looked for them.

b)   Third-Horizon: Contemporary Malawi

Although written originally to an ancient urban audience, using Oakes' model, the socio-historical context of Romans finds clear parallels in contemporary rural Malawi, perhaps closer than to modern Western society.

The Jew-Gentile tensions in Rome are potentially mirrored in Malawian church divisions. This is especially relevant in the towns where there is greater diversity of tribal affiliation, social status, education and wealth than in the villages.[5] There were migrant workers and homeless people in Rome (Oakes 2009, 95) as in Malawian towns. When the conference delegates were asked whether ethnic diversity and tribalism was a problem in the Malawian church,[6] 73 percent agreed, while only 5 percent denied it (40 responses). For example, some congregations, Synods or denominational assemblies exclude people from leadership or membership based on tribe.[7] Delegates responded

---

5. Interview Pastor P1
6. Question 8 of Supplementary Questionnaire/Interview '*Is ethnic diversity and tribalism an issue in the Malawian church? How do pastors deal with it? Could any part of Romans help them with this?*'
7. Delegate D9 (Charismatic Redeemed Ministries International, female; town); Delegate

to tribalism by encouraging equality, inclusiveness and reconciliation, and teaching that judgement and salvation apply to all without favouritism. Just as ancient Roman households generally adopted the religion of their householder, rural Malawians may adhere to the faith of the village chief, or a woman to that of her husband. The picture in Malawi is one of hierarchy, patronage and status.

Paul's desire to consolidate gospel understanding and his apostolic authority in Rome before moving to pioneering mission fields mirrors the need for Bible teaching and practical discipleship in rural Malawian churches before new church planting in villages where ATR or Islam predominate.

Chapter 3 concluded by listing examples of the people that might be found in towns or villages in Malawi. For some, their occupation and social status find parallels within Oakes' model of the Roman house church.

(a) In villages:

- Subsistence farmers and labourers – the unskilled craft worker.
- Landless families given food and shelter in exchange for work – the poor freedman stoneworker and his patron.

(b) In towns:

- Shop or market traders and skilled craft workers – the Roman craft worker
- Manual labourers – the unskilled craft worker
- Beggars without family to support them – the low-status slave

(c) In both locations:

- Wives and widows captive to abuse or prostitution – the exploited slave
- Many children including orphans, carrying water/tending livestock – low-status slave

c) Second-Horizon: Contemporary West

The second-horizon is that of all twenty-first century Western interpreters – distinct from the natural horizons of both Paul and contemporary Malawi. The second-horizon includes all Western contact, direct or indirect, that

D55 (Church of Central Africa, Presbyterian; town); Interview Pastor P4 may interfere with the natural Malawian context, such as Western-style training and non-indigenous church traditions. This includes the author of this book with Western presuppositions that must be laid aside for the interpretative task.

While many Malawian church leaders may read Romans from a natural African traditional viewpoint, others will have had some contact with second-horizon thought forms. This creates the potential for an interpretive gulf between Western influences on the preacher that have not reached the congregation. It is a risk factor that accompanies any non-indigenous training.

4.3   Using Verses in Preaching

In previous surveys of preaching in Malawi, the Letter to the Romans was one of the most-used NT texts after the Gospels and perhaps Acts (section 1.7). This section investigates the factors influencing the use of Romans by provincial-rural preachers.

For analysis, Romans was divided into six chapter blocks: chapter 1, chapters 2–3, chapters 4–6, chapters 7–8, chapters 9–11 and chapters 12–16. The 179 delegates were asked if they had preached recently using each of these blocks, and Yes/No responses were enumerated.

Table 7 shows that slightly over half of delegates had preached from any particular chapter block: more of the experienced pastors had done so (68–84 percent) than inexperienced pastors (60–73 percent) than non-pastors (35–50 percent). Table 8 shows that pastors and non-pastors were more likely to have used Romans if they were trained. The trained pastors used it the most, and untrained non-pastors the least. Figure 1 illustrates the number of different chapter blocks from which any particular delegate had previously preached. Almost every pastor (96 percent) and three-quarters of non-pastors (76 percent) had used Romans at least once. The 12 percent of delegates that had never used Romans were almost entirely untrained non-pastors. Conversely, 34 percent of delegates had preached from all six block of Romans. Pastors that were both trained and experienced were most likely to have used Romans, while interviewing confirmed that untrained lay-leaders, male and female, tended to avoid it.[8]

---

8. Interview Pastor P4

4.4   Reading Romans in Malawi: Popular Verses

Delegates were asked which verses in Romans they had used and what subject they had used them to speak about.[9] The number of Liwonde and Mponela delegates using each verse was plotted on a series of five bar charts (figures 2–6). For each use/sermon, the subject was identified and categorised against the verses used. Further insight into the use of Romans in the Malawian church was gained from written questions and spoken interviews.[10]

From figures 2–6, four individual/pairs of verses were quoted heavily by Malawian preachers. These were:

a)   1:16–17

b)   3:23

c)   10:9–10

d)   12:1–2

Each was cited by over one-sixth of conference delegates (30 or more people). 6:23 was quoted by over one-eighth of delegates (24 people), and is discussed alongside 3:23. Intuitively, these verses are also well used in many UK churches, though often perhaps only as 'proof texts'.

The following sections below discuss each of these passages (a) to (d) separately under the following subheadings:

i)   Existing Use: how the Malawian preachers currently use them.

ii) Between Horizons: exegesis was performed in the first-horizon with emphasis on the OT context, which seems to resonate with African thinking and may help to bridge contexts. The text was then applied in the third-horizon.

a)   *Romans 1:16–17*

i)   Existing Use
56 percent of the 106 delegates that preached from Romans 1 had used verse 16, and 30 percent had used verse 17 (mostly using vv. 16–17 together). 1:16 was the most frequently used verse in Romans.

---

9. Questions 8–13 of basic questionnaire: '*Which verses did you use and what subject did you use them to speak about?*'
10.   Question 2 of supplementary questionnaire/interview: '*How is Romans used in the Malawian church? Which parts are used the most and why?*'

Delegates used verses 16–17 to preach about the power of God (22 delegates), being unashamed of preaching the gospel (19 delegates) and the importance of preaching. A few mentioned salvation being for all – including Gentiles. Sermons therefore focussed on the prominent words in the passage:

- Preaching at any cost, for it is the power of God saving all mankind.[11]

- Christ is calling all nations and he is calling every human being to preach without making shame.[12]

Of those quoting verses 16–17, 80 percent were pastors and 75 percent were trained. The trained pastors seemed especially to like using verse 16 to exhort congregations to be 'shameless' in evangelism like Paul. Fear of shame is a powerful cultural driving force for action in many developing countries. The pastors also encouraged their hearers to depend upon God for power, a desirable resource in Malawi where people often feel powerless to control daily circumstances.[13] Both mainstream churches and AICs preached that salvation is for everyone, including Africans.

ii)   Between Horizons

The second-horizon Protestant Lutheran tradition insists on a judicial, forensic understanding of words that share the δικαιο-root, usually translated "righteousness". However, we must resist the tendency to read Romans only through the spectacles of Western medieval legalism.

There is continuing debate about what Paul meant by δικαιοσύνη θεοῦ in 1:17.[14] He seems to assume his original readers will interpret him successfully, the OT perhaps providing the necessary context. Three important words are linked in 1:16–17: "salvation", "righteousness" and "revealed", as in Psalm 98:2 and Isaiah 56:1. Morris (1988, 102) comments: "the thought in such passages is that God will not abandon his people. Since he is righteous, he will certainly deliver them." Here the LXX meaning of δικαιοσύνη relates to God's character seen in beneficial action, bringing compassionate deliverance. In a dynamic sense, God's righteousness is equivalent to his saving action (Isa 46:13; 51:5–8). There is another more neutral sense of God's righteousness that can be seen in judgement and justice (Ps 50), vindicating the poor and

---

11.   Delegate L1 (Antioch International Church; town)
12.   Delegate L56 on 1:16–17 (Good News Revival Church; village)
13.   A popular worship song is "Lord, give me power, power for every hour".
14.   Also δικαιοσύνη θεοῦ/αὐτοῦ in 3:5, 21, 22, 25, 26; twice in 10:3 and 2 Corinthians 5:21.

afflicted, crushing their oppressors (Moo 1991, 79–80; Grieb 2002, 23). The OT social aspects of δικαιοσύνη are thus active, salvific and covenant relational, epitomized in Psalm 143:1–2. This insight enables all of Romans 1–3 to be read more easily from the viewpoint of the poor person.

The OT understanding was that God's righteousness would be pronounced in salvation only at the final judgement. However, Paul "transfers the final verdict into the present" (Moo 1991, 83–84). He brings forward aspects of final judgement into the "now-time" (1:18–32) using δικαιοσύνη θεοῦ as "an expression for the unity of the eschatological judging and redeeming acts of God" (EDNT 1, 326). While Dunn (1988a, 42) argues that δικαιοσύνη θεοῦ in verse 17 speaks about goodness not justice, it seems at least possible that the γὰρ in verse 18 is a link forward to judgement following logically from justice.

The Malawian notion of 'salvation' may be more practical than in the West, a deliverance from both spiritual and material problems despite challenges from ATR, Islam, poverty, sickness or death. Indeed, σωτηρία (salvation) is used in the LXX to depict deliverance from a range of evils as well as eschatological salvation (Moo 1991, 61).

Thus, Paul speaks of δικαιοσύνη θεοῦ in Romans with "focus on redemptive action" (BDAG, 247). However, θεοῦ is not necessarily exclusively a genitive of origin – righteousness *from* God – which can signify a new legal status given to people by God. While the issues surrounding this phrase are complex (Moo 1991, 77), it can be argued that righteousness is a dynamic attribute of impartial justice (putting things right for the poor and oppressed) and saving covenant faithfulness (offering hope and restoration to the downtrodden). This concurs with the Western 'New Perspective' definition of δικαιοσύνη θεοῦ as "God's faithful covenant justice" (Wright 2005, 32).

Oakes reads 1:16–17 from the perspective of an oppressed Roman slave. He remarks, "for most people in the world, the need for justice is probably a bigger perceived issue than the need for forgiveness . . . justice must be a central element of God's righteousness" (2009, 133). For Malawian Christians forced to initiate into Nyau, houses destroyed in witch-hunts, wives infected with HIV/AIDS through adultery or abused because of drunkenness, and widows denied inheritance rights by greedy relatives[15] – injustice may be their main felt concern. The knowledge that the gospel has power to deliver anyone who believes is a key aspect of their 'salvation'. For the faithful, there is need

---

15.   All situations described by Interview Pastor P1

to be declared righteous, to receive personal forgiveness and gain freedom from guilt, yet also to receive a divine promise of justice and declaration of judgement against oppressors. This incarnates the gospel as 'good news' for them in their particular situation.

b)   *Romans 3:23 and 6:23*

i)   Existing Use

32 percent of the 111 delegates who preached from Romans 2–3 had used 3:23. They were predominantly pastors (78 percent) and trained (75 percent). Delegates used 3:23 to preach on 'sin' (17 delegates), emphasizing its importance for contemporary Malawian society:

- I preached against sin of our culture we are practicing.[16]

- [Sin] it's everyone's concern.[17]

In interviews, pastors mentioned involvement in witchcraft and polygamy as practical examples of sin. The theological term 'original sin' was raised by three delegates from missionary-instituted denominations,[18] two having previously trained full-time. 'Original sin' imposes a theological category which is never used anywhere in the Bible. This illustrates how Western training curricula may lead to Malawians adopting presuppositions alien to the natural thinking of their congregations.

Delegates had preached about prominent theological words in the passage, like 'salvation', 'redemption', 'grace' and 'freedom' (16 delegates):

- We were redeemed through the death of Jesus on the cross.[19]

- God's grace has set us free.[20]

These topics have potential for African contextual interpretation.

The δικαιο-root words 'Justification' and 'God's righteousness' – however these might be understood contextually – were nevertheless discussed only by a few well-trained delegates, seemingly in Western theological terms:

---

16.   Delegate D108 on 3:23 (Assemblies of God; town)
17.   Delegate L36 on 3:23 (Assemblies of God; trading-centre)
18.   Delegate L92 on 3:23 (Evangelical Baptist Church of Malawi, female; town); Delegate L95 on 3:23 (Church of Central Africa, Presbyterian, female; town); Delegate D86 on 3:23 (Anglican; village)
19.   Delegate D8 on 3:23–24 (Assemblies Movement Church; village)
20.   Delegate L75 on 3:21–24 (Good Samaritan Church; town)

- Righteousness through Christ our only Saviour. Fall of man, salvation as a gift.[21]

A senior pastor observed: "Most who have not studied theology will not touch justification by faith";[22] other theological topics in 3:21–26, like atonement, were likewise not highlighted.

3:23–24 were used mostly to formulate simple gospel messages about sin, salvation and God's glory, without contextual interpretation:

- All people are sinful and they are saved through Jesus Christ.[23]

- How we can go through to the glory of God?[24]

6:22–23 were used similarly to proclaim sin, repentance, salvation and eternal life/death:

- Jesus is calling all people to repent, fearing the cost of sin is hell.[25]

- Sin brings death but Jesus brings life.[26]

An AIC pastor said of 6:23: "The one who does good things will receive good things, and vice versa."[27] While Western interpretations might, at first, hear in this a works-based salvation, this expresses a practical African and indeed OT Biblical understanding that doing good and receiving God's blessing are interconnected.

Romans 3:23 and 6:23 are thus widely quoted verses in rural Malawi. They are sometimes used to teach about the socio-cultural and theological aspects of sin, but more especially as 'proof texts' in evangelistic messages on salvation – as intuitively happens also in the UK. Contextualisation is dominated by theological categories, with little evidence that the passage is being read against the life concerns of rural Malawi.

ii)   Between Horizons

The language of 3:21–26 is dominated by δικαιο-root words, variously translated 'righteousness', 'justice', 'just' and 'justify'. In 1:16–17, we saw that reading Romans in both first- and third-horizons required God's judgement be viewed as part of the 'good news' of salvation. 'Righteousness' was not

---

21.   Delegate D58 on 3:21–31 (Church of Central Africa, Presbyterian; village)
22.   Interview Pastor P3
23.   Delegate D47 on 3:22–24 (Baptist Church; village)
24.   Delegate D13 on 3:23 (Living Waters Church; village)
25.   Delegate L56 on 6:23 (Good News Revival Church; village)
26.   Delegate D86 on 6:23 (Anglican Church; village)
27.   Delegate L45 on 6:22–23 (Calvary Family Church, female; trading-centre)

only revealed (3:21) in order to be received *from* God in counterpoint to his wrath (negatively), but was an attribute *of* God to assure the downtrodden (positively) there will be a "day when God will judge men's secrets" (2:16). God as just creator must one day put the world to rights. By this reading, 1:18–3:20 does more than simply set up a context of need for redemption in 3:21and following.

Although 3:23 is a much quoted verse, it is not the main proposition of 3:21–24, but an elaboration of verse 22b "there is no difference" between Jew and Gentile (Moo 1991, 226). The identical position of "all people" before God explains the main idea of the paragraph, which is that δικαιοσύνη θεοῦ has been revealed "now" (v. 21a). In the original first-horizon context of Jew-Gentile tension and Paul's desire to re-establish unity, this tragic backdrop of universal sinfulness reaffirms that there is no ground for superiority between any groups or individuals. In Roman society, glory belonged visibly to the elite. Yet the status of Emperor and slave, Jew and Gentile, rich and poor, oppressor and downtrodden, are equalized beneath "all have sinned" (v. 23).

The word 'Redemption' (ἀπολύτρωσις; v. 24) resonates with the Roman world of commerce and slavery (BDAG, 117). For the house-church members, especially slaves, redemption was the process through which they might gain freedom (manumission). It is by redemption in Christ that δικαιοσύνη θεοῦ was activated in their lives by grace (v. 24) to bring deliverance from troubles. For the oppressed in Rome (and rural Malawi), δικαιοσύνη justice (1:17; 3:25–26) and ἀπολύτρωσις freedom (3:24) are essential ingredients of any contextual notion of 'salvation'.

In Malawi, there is a passion for evangelistic 'gospel' preaching now seen rarely in the UK. However, preachers may use 3:23 only as a 'proof text' for the universality of sin. Yet, its wider literary context of verses 21–26 ties this verse into pragmatic themes of equality, freedom and justice. To do this may increase the impact of the gospel in oppressed communities, and help develop an enduring Christian discipleship rooted in African contextual theology rather than imported from the West.

3:23 creates an opening for church leaders to teach about sin using practical illustrations from Malawian life. Sin is variously caused by moral ignorance and/or disobedience. Some require education, others persuasion. Examples of sin might be congregational involvement in witchcraft, traditional medicine, ancestor rites and Nyau/Islam, sexual/marital issues and relationship problems. Tribal and familial superiority in society because of wealth, employment or gender, and in churches/denominations may be addressed by teaching the equality of all before God – both under the slavery of sin (3:23) and the freedom of grace (3:24). Although nineteenth century African slavery differed from that in Roman society, its legacy in Malawi may give life to Paul's enslavement imagery (6:15–23). Superior and boastful attitudes are "excluded" (v. 27) in Christ, because theologically all have shared the death of a slave (6:6), and now all live the life of a son (8:14–16). 3:23 provides the theological foundation for the practical assertion (12:3) that no one may have an overinflated self-opinion.

c)   *Romans 10:9–10*

i)   Existing Use

39 percent of the 95 delegates that preached from Romans 9–11 had used 10:9, (34 percent using vv. 9–10 together). 10:9–10 were well used compared with other parts of chapters 9–11, which generally were among the least used in the letter.

Delegates mainly used verses 9–10 to reiterate the two-fold exhortation to "believe in your heart" (24 delegates) and "confess with your mouth" (13 delegates):

- If anyone believe and say yes to Jesus he/she will be saved.[28]

- Confess that Jesus is the Lord.[29]

Some delegates used these verses to teach that salvation is for everyone equally, drawing on former Jews-Gentiles distinctions to illustrate:

- We, the Gentiles, are also saved by Jesus the same as the Jews.[30]

- Great and universal salvation both for Israel and Gentiles.[31]

Interviewing revealed that many pastors traditionally use 10:9–10 at Christian funerals to appeal for unbelievers in the village to convert to Christ.[32] They advocate a simple conversion call (heart response plus verbal confession), accessible to anyone including the illiterate. These two verses were widely used in Malawi by mainstream and AICs, Pentecostal and evangelical denominations, trained and untrained preachers to encourage publically

---

28.   Delegate L56 on 10:9–10 (Apostolic Faith Mission; village)
29.   Delegate D39 on 10:5–10 (Church of Central Africa, Presbyterian; village)
30.   Delegate L25 on 9:14–24 and 10:9–12 and 11:7–12 (Victory Pentecostal Church; village)
31.   Delegate D58 on chapters 9–11 (Church of Central Africa, Presbyterian; village)
32.   Interview Pastor P1

expressed Christian commitment and support a distinctive Christian identity within traditional rural society.

ii)   Between Horizons

In the Roman house churches, there would likely have been both Jewish and Gentile Christians represented, as Oakes suggests. Paul was writing with some angst in chapters 9–11 to a situation where most Hellenistic Jews had rejected the gospel message, and the Jewish Christians were a minority within a largely Gentile-dominated church.

The context of verses 9–10 is verses 6–8, where God's OT "word" of command is declared accessibly and understandably (Deut 9:4 and 30:12–14). God was speaking this "word" through Paul to the Roman church, but now one of "righteousness from faith" (10:6). This translation of δικαιοσύνη ἐκ πίστεως retains a sense of both God's covenant faithfulness and the need for human response of faith (Dunn 1988b, 602).

What was this 'word' in verses 9–10? 'Confess' (ὁμολογέω) implies a solemn act of public profession of allegiance. 'Believe' (πιστεύω) refers to "a faith that takes hold of the whole of the inner man" (Morris 1988, 385). Such verbs would have resonated in the daily lives of house-church members living under household and imperial authority and benefactor-client patronage.

Furthermore, the term 'lord' (κύριος) was used among Gentiles to refer to pagan deities or the Emperor (Morris 1988, 385). To ancient Romans it was only a small step from exalting the Emperor as a human to identifying him with the gods; people were expected to venerate the image of the Emperor as a sign of loyalty to the state (Jeffers 2002, 129). Dunn comments: "κύριος was widely used to denote an asserted or acknowledged dominance and right of disposal of superior over inferior. So to confess someone as 'lord' denotes an attitude of subservience and sense of belonging or devotion to the one so named" (1988b, 608). Yet, κύριος was used among Jews extensively for the name of God (LXX). The declaration in 10:9–10 thus functions as a Christian "slogan of identification" (Dunn 1988b, 607) equivalent to Deuteronomy 6:4 for OT Israel. It is a public confession of Christ's deity. Though Paul asserts that human hierarchies are equalized before God regarding sin and grace (3:23–24), Christ alone is κύριος.

There are good pragmatic reasons to encourage public verbal declaration of Christian faith in Malawi. In many rural locations, new converts are required by pastors to declare their Christian faith openly and verbally to the village chief and local community. This step is viewed as the only sure guarantee of protection from the social and cultural demands of ATR, especially *Gule Wamkulu*.[33]

In conclusion, in the first-horizon readers might read this verse in patron-client terms, with God not Caesar as benefactor. In the third-horizon, Malawians may likewise view God as their benefactor delivering protection and security in exchange for demonstrable public loyalty in making such declarations.

d)   *Romans 12:1–2*

i)   Existing Use

32 percent of the 115 delegates that preached from Romans 12–16 used 12:1, and 29 percent used 12:2 (26 percent using 12:1–2 together). 83 percent of those using verses 1–2 were pastors and 75 percent were trained, a similar pattern to 1:16–17 and 3:23.

Delegates used verses 1–2 to preach about being "living sacrifices" (19 delegates) through devotion to God:

- Real sacrifice. Keep understanding important ways about loving God and serving him with our whole body.[34]

- Doing things which are not enough to God like giving a dead sacrifice.[35]

Some delegates used these verses to teach about transformation and renewal of the heart and mind (8 delegates):

- Change of mind.[36]

- Transformation in one's heart.[37]

A few used verses 1–2 to introduce the broader theme in Romans 12–15 of "practising the Christian life"[38] Sermons generally focussed on key words in the text like 'sacrifice', 'body' and 'mind'.

---

33.   Interview Pastor P1
34.   Delegate L36 on 12:1–2 (Assemblies of God; trading-centre)
35.   Delegate L4 on chapter 12 (Good News Revival Church; town)
36.   Delegate D106 on 12:1–2 (Victory Pentecostal Church; town)
37.   Delegate D29 on 12:1–3 (Assemblies of God; town)
38.   Delegate D104 on chapters 12–15 (Assemblies of God; town)

ii)   Between Horizons

In Romans chapters 1–11, Paul explains God's salvation with little application.[39] From 12:1 onwards, he begins a thorough call for ethical action "in view of God's mercies". While verses 1–2 deals with attitude to God, verses 3–16 speaks of attitude to other people.

12:1 introduce the theme of 'sacrifice'. Oakes (2009, 99) outlines how craft workers in the Roman house churches may have belonged to trade associations, whose communal meals included short token sacrifices to their patron's deity. Roman households may have offered token sacrifice rituals on special family occasions such as childbirth and funerals, while those working in domestic service or slavery may have participated in domestic cults. The culture was probably familiar to many house-church members.

Paul however, contrasts such token sacrifice rites with the response of total sacrifice to God required by gospel living. The believer is to be a living, thinking sacrifice, perhaps by contrast with the dead unthinking animals of OT sacrifices (Morris 1988, 434). Everyone in the church provides living sacrifices as a continuing act of devotion. Craft workers could meaningfully offer their bodies as "tools of righteousness" (6:13). Even exploited slaves, lacking possessions and whose bodies were owned by others, could offer their actions.

In Malawi, it is compulsory for the whole community to attend village funerals. Not to do so brings shame and may attract a fine from the chiefs.[40] Many are pressured to participate in food sacrifices at ceremonies like *sadaka*, *chinamwali* and *Gule Wamkulu*. It is hard for Christians to resist involvement in these 'token sacrifices', yet they draw people away from the life of total sacrifice to Christ.

The exhortation to "offer your body" (v. 1) has implications not only for village prostitutes, but also for sexual practices generally in Malawi. Many village women will have had their bodies involuntarily taken and repeatedly used by men since they were young. For example, the sexually initiated young woman who believes she has no choice but to respond positively to any proposition; the married woman who feels she must obey whatever her husband demands; the rape victim who was ambushed in the fields or attacked while collecting water; and the prostitute seeking to support her

---

39.   Only in 6:12–13; 6:19 and 11:20
40.   Interview Pastor P1

family. The invitation for them to "offer" their bodies as holy to God could be liberating as they struggle with self worth.

Many rural Malawians, living in poverty, have a sense that nothing will ever change in their lives. The instructions "do not conform . . . but be transformed . . ." (v. 2) challenges this assumption. They must live differently from those around them who refuse to be "living sacrifices". For example, town traders must handle money honestly; women must speak truthfully and not gossip; a man must be kind and faithful to his wife and children. "Renewing of your mind" means no longer to think like an unbeliever. It does not demand great education, but the moral approach to conversion, which is commonly found in Malawi. The popularity of this verse is matched by its wide-ranging potential applicability to Malawian life.

4.5   Discussion

Chapter 4 begins the process of interpreting Romans from its ancient first-horizon to the third-horizon of contemporary rural Malawi. On many occasions, this African horizon seems potentially nearer to Paul's original context than the Western understanding of the second-horizon interpreter. Considering these verses and their literary contexts between these horizons helps understand how rural Malawians could receive these verses.

The chapter identifies several individual/pairs of verses that are highly popular in Malawian preaching: Romans 1:16–17; 3:23–24; 6:23; 10:9–10; 12:1–2. The first four are frequently used as part of an evangelistic gospel presentation, and often without reference to the surrounding literary context. Except for 10:9–10, they are used particularly by pastors who have received training and are experienced in ministry. They are less well-used by lay leaders, pastors in their early years of ministry, and those without training. These verses contain some difficult key terms that those who have been trained may be more willing to consider. Perhaps their very overfamiliarity makes it harder for Malawian preachers to view them culturally.

Many Western congregations also quote these much-beloved verses. Collectively they encapsulate a superficial gospel of salvation and devotion in both contexts. Admittedly, legalistic righteousness and marketplace redemption are not to be denied efficacy anywhere. Yet the image of salvation projected in third-horizon Malawi should bear some contextual marks to differentiate it from that of the Western second-horizon. The greater felt needs in Malawi may in fact be salvific justice, covenant faithfulness and redemptive freedom for the oppressed. In the next chapter we will look at paragraphs of Romans to see how the interpretative agenda may be further shaped by the contextual needs of rural Malawi.

5

Romans and Ministry

5.1 Introduction

Chapter 4 offers contextual interpretation of the five most popular individual/pairs of *verses* in Romans. This chapter continues the contextual reading of Romans by identifying the most used and least used *paragraphs* of Romans (section 5.2). Selected paragraphs are then read against the socio-cultural and pastoral issues in the third-horizon context (section 5.3). The following topics are discussed:

a) Faith and Ancestors amidst Backsliding (4:1–15 and 5:12–21)

b) Circumcision amidst Islam/Traditional Rituals (2:25–29)

c) Marriage amidst Marital problems (7:1–6)

d) Assurance amidst Suffering (8:14–17)

e) Compassion amidst Poverty (12:3–21)

5.2 Using Paragraphs in Preaching

Table 9 shows the paragraphs of Romans (defined statistically as a group of six or more consecutive verses) that were most used by delegates in their preaching. These blocks of text were: 1:8–15; 2:2–9; 4:1–8; 6:1–15; 8:1–17; 8:31–39; 10:1–15 and 12:1–21. It is important to recognize that even these most-used paragraphs were quoted by fewer preachers (6–13 percent of delegates) than any of the popular verses (18–33 percent of delegates) discussed in chapter 4. This analysis therefore only offers an indication of the paragraphs of Romans used by a minority of provincial-rural Malawian preachers.

Table 10 shows the paragraphs of Romans that were least-used by delegates in preaching. These were: 3:1–8; 5:12–21; 8:18–30; 9:1–13; 9:16–33; 11:11–36 and 14:1–16:27. This gives an indication of the sections that are rarely or never used by preachers. When delegates were asked why some parts of Romans are rarely used,[1] some ascribed personal reasons such as 'laziness'[2] or 'living a carnal life'.[3] But often, delegates simply chose to preach from easier, more familiar stories:[4]

- They just run to the familiar stories.[5]

- There are usual verses a pastor may find easier to prepare a message from.[6]

Others delegates verbalized the difficulties they experienced in finding a shared understanding between the original context of Romans and that of contemporary Malawi:

- Not many preachers are conversant with the meaning of some of the words, culture of the Jews and some historical facts. So they prefer straightforward verses.[7]

- Most denominations prohibit some things, and they assume [Romans] is not inspired by the Holy Spirit because it does not speak according to their understanding.[8]

A trained, non-pastor summarized the discomfort poorly educated Malawian preachers experience with Paul's writings:

- Some chapters [of Romans] are rarely used because they are difficult to interpret. Bearing in mind only 5 percent of Malawian pastors are educated, the remaining percentage face problems in exegeting the context, so concentrate on Synoptic Gospels and Old Testament. Many preachers feel it is difficult to relate the Pauline letters to current salvation, hence they just ignore them.[9]

---

1. Question 3 of the Supplementary Questionnaire/Interview: 'Are some parts of Romans used only rarely? Why not more often?'
2. Delegate D85 (Living Waters Church, female non-pastor; trading-centre)
3. Delegate D1 (Assemblies of God; trading-centre)
4. Delegate L16 (Church of Central Africa, Presbyterian; village)
5. Delegate D85 (Living Waters Church, female non-pastor; trading-centre)
6. Delegate D9 (Charismatic Redeemed Ministries International, female pastor; town)
7. Delegate L73 (Church of Central Africa, Presbyterian; town)
8. Delegate L53 (Zambezi Evangelical Church; town)
9. Delegate L30 (Assemblies of God; village)

This quotation hints at discontinuity between the meaning of salvation understood in Paul's first-horizon writings, and in the natural third-horizon of Malawian villages, as mediated directly or indirectly to them by Western and/or non-Western interpreters.

Yet, difficulty in understanding Romans is not uniquely African. We can only ever partially reconstruct Paul's first-horizon meaning. Second-horizon interpretations have emerged from this in various Western contexts, and are neither uniform, nor static. The New Perspective interpretations (pioneered by Sanders, Stendahl, Dunn and Wright) have been applied in fresh ways to Romans, for example in the work of Grieb (2002) and Oakes (2009). These interpretations have emerged in recent decades entirely within Western contexts, as an alternative to the old Lutheran understandings. Such debates over interpretation address linguistic, theological or textual issues, as in the 'pistis christou' debate (Bird, 2010).

Many delegates underlined the need to be trained in interpretation. However, trainers must be careful not to impose answers to questions that the Malawian preachers have never asked or owned. The second-horizon must avoid creating barriers to development of genuine third-horizon contextual interpretations from Paul's first-horizon message.

5.3   Reading Romans in Malawi: Paragraphs

In this section, the interpretation of Romans is arranged topically. The issues faced by churches are highlighted, the existing use of some paragraphs by Malawian preachers is described, and contextual interpretations are discussed in the interpretative horizons.

a)   Faith and Ancestors amidst Backsliding (4:1–15 and 5:12–21)

i)   Existing Use
Delegates highlighted "backsliding through lack of faith" as the precursor of sinful behaviour and return to traditional religion. They said: "[People] need illustrations of those who travelled and did not backslide."[10] Romans chapter 4 was overwhelmingly understood to speak about faith and righteousness: the power, consequences, blessings and fruit of faith were taught from verses 1–8 (17 delegates). Paul appeals to different aspects of the OT narrative of

---

10.   Conference Discussion Group feedback

Abraham (Gen 12–25) as a running test case, a concrete example of such a faith-journey.

Malawi has a culture of story telling, so Paul's use of the OT Abraham narratives should help Malawian readers to see faith through real-life actions. Theological principles and practical expression of faith are closely linked. Delegates taught Abraham's active faith in the face of childlessness using 4:18– 25. In rural Malawi, childlessness is a source of shame, practical difficulty in old age, and a common reason for people turning aside to traditional medicine. In a Contextual Bible Study, God's 'faithfulness', working out through the faith of Abraham, was perceived as the solution to the problem: "what God says, he does."[11] Wright concurs from a Western 'New Perspective' standpoint, "God has made promises; Israel can trust those promises. God's righteousness is thus cognate with his trustworthiness on one hand and Israel's salvation on the other" (Wright 1997, 96).

The Patriarchs are well regarded by many in the Malawian church – some African-initiated denominations even use their lifestyles to validate polygamy traditions within their own culture. Awareness of tribal roots and ancestral stories is important in Malawi. As "father of many nations" (4:18), delegates suggested Abraham was a key 'ancestor' of anyone who has faith – whether Jews, Gentiles or Africans.[12] Yet some preachers validated only biological links to the Patriarchs, hence not relevant to Africans:

- Malawians are not direct descendants of Patriarchs, their salvation is not by law and promises to the Patriarchs, but their salvation as Gentiles should come by faith and good works.[13]

Indeed, some Western missionaries refute any theological compatibility whatsoever between Christianity and the ancestors (Gehman 1989, 184). These second-horizon views could reduce the receptivity of delegates in the third-horizon to an ancestor metaphor for Abraham. Furthermore, ancestors (at least within Chewa society) are only thought capable of engaging with their own matrilineal group (VanBreugal 2001, 74), which might increase felt irrelevance in the third-horizon.

Paul speaks of the solidarity of mankind with Adam in 5:12–21. Adam could be viewed as our basal ancestor, with whom everyone including Africans shares socio-ethnic solidarity. Yet 5:12–21 was one of the least-used paragraphs

---

11.   Deacon in Contextual Bible Study (Assemblies of God)
12.   Deacon in Contextual Bible Study (Assemblies of God)
13.   Delegate L32 (Roman Catholic; village)

by delegates (4 delegates), only one pastor speaking in representative terms of Adam sinning "for all", and Jesus "saving all".[14] Malawians seem not to embrace Adam as easily as they do Abraham. Maybe Paul's comparison of Adam and Christ lacks felt relevance. While Abraham's actions are positive (of faith), Adam's are negative (of sin and death). A deceased Malawian is unlikely to be granted ancestor status if they were spoken of in such negative terms as Adam. Furthermore, Western interpreters may have introduced doubt or confusion by communicating their own rationalist struggle over solidarity with a literal Adam. Perhaps the Malawian preachers are simply avoiding Paul's theological intricacy.

ii) Between Horizons

In Romans 4, there is an emphasis on continuity of promise from Abraham to the reader (Moo 1988, 270), potentially making Abraham seem a good ancestor for Africans to emulate. Abraham offers concrete expression to δικαιοσύνη θεοῦ, seen through God's power working actively in his life. Paul introduces the notion of δικαιοσύνη θεοῦ in 1:16–17 and develops it throughout Romans 1–3 (section 4.4). In the Malawian church, if Christianity is not seen to be 'working', bringing solutions to their problems, people may modify their faith allegiance, perhaps returning to magic, traditional medicine and witchcraft. Christian faith needs likewise to be seen to work in post-modern Western expectations.

In the first-horizon, Paul highlighted the social distinctiveness of Jews and Gentiles in 1:16–17, yet affirmed that salvation is for both equally. He stated that "there is no difference" (3:22–23) with respect to δικαιοσύνη before God, so neither group can judge the other (2:1–3) or boast superiority (3:27). In Romans 4, Paul describes the significance of Abraham's OT faith and God's faithfulness in his life – and by extension the same in the lives of his readers. In 4:3, Paul uses Abraham's practical believing back in Genesis 15:6 as a template for all now having equal access to being declared 'righteous' (δικαιόω) by faith.

Faith (πίστις) may be characterised as a "state of believing on the basis of the reliability of the one trusted" (BDAG, 818–819). God was 'the One' whom Abraham trusted. Paul argues such faith differs from works (ἔργα), which demonstrate the reality of faith (4:19–20; 10:10; 12:6; 14:2). Paul assumes his readers understand what he means by ἔργα, as he did for δικαιοσύνη. In recent

---

14. Delegate L79 (Christ Citadel International; town)

years, this has created fierce debate in Western circles between traditional 'old perspective' readings, which view works negatively as self-merit in opposition to faith, and the covenantal nomism (Sanders) of the 'new perspective' which perceive them as social boundary markers of Jewish identity (particularly circumcision, food laws and Sabbath-keeping). In this view, works are to keep Israel within the covenant, not demark its entry points. The revisionists claim Luther projected his medieval context back onto the first century, while their own views set works into their first-century context (Dunn 2006, 179–180). However, it seems both agendas risk interfering with the historic meaning when they bring the text into a radically different context like Malawi.

In the third-horizon, Mijoga (2003, 6) interprets works through its OT background, which he argues Paul's original first-horizon readers would also have understood (Gen 18:19; Deut 17:11). As a Malawian theologian, albeit Western-influenced, he suggests works imply activity, that faith is realized through verbs like "do, keep, uphold and remember" in relation to the (Jewish) law (Mijoga, 2003:7). In summary, faith in Malawi needs a demonstrable ethical component evidenced through a changed life.

In provincial-rural Malawi, 4:1–8 together with 6:1–15 could be used to connect faith with righteous living and blessing. This might be delivered through Contextual Bible Studies with interest groups like young people preparing for transition to adulthood. Consideration of life as a faith journey requiring e.g. to reject ATR/Muslim practices, witchcraft and magic, beer-culture and domestic violence, but rather to embrace honesty with money, sexual abstinence before marriage, fidelity within it, and patient hope. Reading this through Malawian eyes, one delegate said:

- Paul talked of having faith in Jesus . . . so there is no need of trusting the witch-doctors.[15]

As noted previously, 'born again' conversion may be expressed in rural Malawi as a change of practice more than belief (Mangos, 2010). For Malawian Christians, the biggest challenge is to keep faithful, like Abraham (4:20–21), despite facing life's difficulties.

Finally, ancestral spirits play a vital role in traditional Malawian thought, being frequently granted supernatural status, a mediating role between people and God, and an exemplary role to emulate. Adam is man's eponymous ancestor, the father of the human tribe who revealed sin and

---

15.   Delegate L73 (Church of Central Africa, Presbyterian; town)

death – but he is scarcely exemplary (5:15–16). Christ is the "new Adam", the 'proto-ancestor' who models sinlessness and brings life (Bujo 1992, 82). This contextual analogy may help Malawians relate better to the notion of Christ, the soteriological 'first-born' among all the ancestors, and to believe that power is available in Christ to live a righteous life.

b)   Circumcision amidst Islam/Traditional Rituals (2:25–29)

i)   Existing Use

Traditional Malawian village life is subject to rituals at every stage: birth, *chinamwali*, circumcision and funeral. Non-observance is often considered a potential cause of death or disaster to themselves or others, and hence a matter for community discipline. In Nyau, rituals become captive religion. These practices are a source of fear, and a challenge to the church. As discussed above, some churches attempt to Christianize such rituals (section 3.3b). In this section, we will consider circumcision rituals.

'Circumcision' was a Muslim challenge to Liwonde churches, and a feature of Nyau initiations in Mponela. For church members to enter into non-Christian circumcision rituals was seen as valueless and deeply concerning by church leaders:

- Muslims do circumcision as a sign of righteousness. So where are we putting ourselves if we use it as a sign of righteousness?[16]

Although 2:25–29 speaks of circumcision, it was little used in preaching (6 delegates). Delegates pointed out that circumcision/uncircumcision was not the important distinctive, but having Christ.[17] Although concern over the impact of Muslim circumcision was high, engagement with Jewish circumcision in relation to the law (2:25–29) or Abraham and his faith (4:10) was low.

ii)   Between Horizons

Jewish circumcision was an issue in the first-century church, as Muslim circumcision is in contemporary Malawi. The integration of Muslim circumcision practices into churches was perceived as a threat by the Liwonde leaders, an invasion of Islamic works-righteousness into the church. In traditional Western interpretations of Romans, Paul dismisses circumcision

---

16.   Deacon in Contextual Bible Study (Assemblies of God)
17.   Delegate D35 on topic 'circumcision' (Assemblies of God; trading-centre)

as a means to achieve works-righteousness by merit. By this reading, Paul is drawing adversative contrast in 9:30–10:4 between non-Christian Jews focussed on the narrow rules of law and ethnicity, and Christian Gentiles now submitting to the broader demand of faith. Those preachers in the third-horizon that share this second-horizon understanding of Paul may here find Biblical arguments for rejecting Muslim circumcision. This argument could be extended to not accepting Ramadan sacrificial goats or indeed any ritual practices of ATR/folk religion that ultimately symbolize works-righteousness.

What about 'Christianized circumcision' as an alternative to traditional transition rites? Paul affirmed in his earlier Galatian letter, probably known to the Roman church, "in Christ Jesus neither circumcision nor uncircumcision has any value. The only thing that counts is faith expressing itself through love" (Gal 5:6).[18] In 4:10, Abraham was not circumcised at birth, but only as a subsequent seal of his faith calling.

In summary, Malawian Christians should not expect to seal their faith by works-righteousness rituals, but by the "circumcised heart" (2:29)[19] of living a godly life.

c)   Marriage and Marital problems (7:1–6)

i)   Existing Use

Christian marriage is threatened by traditional practices like polygamy, oppressive and violent male behaviour and adultery, leading to HIV/AIDS, resentment and divorce. Women may be physically and sexually abused during marriage and denied inheritances after their husbands have died. In the villages especially, poorly educated, unattached women cannot easily live independently, and so may be taken as additional wives to assist with housework or farm labouring.

Some delegates recognised the husband-wife relationship in 7:1–6 was an analogy. With or without reference to the theological themes of the paragraph, they spiritualised the marriage paradigm through the cultural lens of a wife obeying instructions – the prevalent culture in rural Malawi:

- We were married in Jesus Christ and . . . are supposed to follow him and obey.[20]

---

18.   Also Galatians 6:15; 1 Corinthians 7:19.
19.   Delegate D26 on 2:25–29 (Living Waters Church; town)
20.   Delegate L88 on 7:1–3 (Apostolic Faith Mission; town)

- Only Jesus should direct our actions.[21]

Others read the text literally as instructions on the nature and conduct of marriage itself:

- Marriage covenant stands as long as partners live and even when separated.[22]
- Both men and women should take care of each other.[23]

There was indeed no "universal perspective" (Ukpong 2002, 17) on the meaning of the text.

ii)   Between Horizons

Paul uses marriage as an example in 7:1–6 to prove a relevant theological argument – that by death within a past relationship to law (probably Jewish Law) the believer is freed to enter a new relationship with Christ. It is inconceivable that Paul intended, or his Roman audience heard, verses 1–6 as teaching on the ethics of marriage, divorce and remarriage.[24] This is a contemporary preoccupation imposed onto Paul's ancient world.

Yet, in the worldview of rural Malawi, the imagery of marriage seems to resonate so powerfully that the illustration acquires a new existence outside the constraints of its original contexts. When Malawian pastors use this paragraph to address issues of polygamy, adultery and widowhood, they mine new meanings in their natural third-horizon by radical reader response. Here, Paul has palpably lost control over how the words are being read.

How might Paul have understood the allegory in verses 2–3? His emphasis fits with the Jewish background, where wives had no right to divorce husbands, but husbands could divorce wives (Deut 24:1–4), and wives were free from marriage only upon the husband's death (Schreiner 1998, 347). In 7:2, Paul speaks of a legally married woman (ὕπανδρος γυνὴ), the word that is used in the LXX to translate 'married'.

In his main argument, Paul says the law exercises lordship over (κυριεύω) a person (7:1). The same verb is used of the lordship of sin and death in 6:9 and 6:14. Dunn calls this situation: "a baneful thing, a mark of man's bondage" (1988a, 359). In the marriage analogy (7:2), the married woman is likewise

---

21.   Delegate L43 on 7:1–6 (Evangelical Baptist Church of Malawi; town)
22.   Delegate D101 on 7:1–6 (Pentecostal Church, female non-pastor; village)
23.   Delegate L73 on 7:1–6 (Church of Central Africa, Presbyterian; town)
24.   Issues of marriage and widows are explicitly addressed elsewhere in the Pauline corpus (1 Cor 7; 1 Tim 5).

bound (δέω) to the husband, and ὕπανδρος carries the literal connotation "under the power of, or subject to a man" (BDAG, 1029), or "subordinated to a man" (EDNT, 3.395). In 7:5, the word commonly translated "sinful passions" (πάθημα) may alternatively be rendered as "that which is suffered or endured" (BADG, 747). This allegorical married woman is regarded as the passive receptor of painful experiences (Morris 1988, 274). "The flesh" (σάρξ) can mean a "power sphere" where someone lives (Moo 1991, 442–443), a place where things happen to parts of the body (μέλος). These word images connote the husband physically controlling the wife and her body. Grieb (2002, 69) argues Paul is suggesting "the situation of a married woman is comparable to a slave".

In Malawi, this image of the married woman resonates with the life experiences of many Malawian village women – obliged to work in the home and the fields during the day, and to satisfy the demands of their husbands at night. What opportunity for escape do they have? Divorce is not mentioned within the analogy, and would not seem to be Paul's intention (Moo 1991, 446). But the text does speak about remarriage being adultery while the first husband still lives. Furthermore, if the illustration could be reversed (i.e. by applying the remarriage to men), then it might be used to refute polygamy. These are significant practical and ethical problems inside and outside the Malawian church.

In 7:2–3, the marriage illustration says "the death of a spouse sets the other spouse 'free from' the law that brands a second marriage as adulterous" (Moo 1991, 435). One pastor said it is common for relatives to lay claim to a widow and her property, leaving her homeless and destitute. While he acknowledged this was not Paul's original purpose of the passage, this pastor purposefully used verses 2–3 to contend on behalf of a vulnerable widow that her marriage had legally ended at death, and she was now free of obligations toward the male blood relatives of her late husband.[25]

In conclusion, Paul's illustration from marriage finds power and relevance in the third-horizon through the key word 'marriage' (as likewise does the key word 'baptism' in 6:4). Yet there is always a danger of abusing analogies by squeezing more meaning from them than the author intended. This is surely happening here. The use is inductive, radical reader response even. However, the resulting teaching is ethically Biblical and within this community of

---

25.   Interview Pastor P1

faith seemingly "it works", potentially bringing transformation. Can we not therefore view it positively?

d)   *Assurance amidst Suffering (8:1–39)*

i)   Existing Use

Suffering, poverty and disease are endemic in rural Malawi. Villages in particular are characterised by lack of basic amenities, healthcare and balanced nutrition. One-seventh of Malawian children are orphans, often due to HIV/AIDS. Most village families exist by subsistence farming and labouring, with incomes under £1/day and no financial cushion against problems. Yet Malawian Christians can be shallow rooted in their faith, seeking security in traditional medicine and consulting ancestors through magicians and diviners.

Delegates overwhelmingly understood Romans 8 to show how the Holy Spirit assists people in suffering and weakness.[26] The Holy Spirit was supremely important to many delegates, engaging an African worldview of many spirits. In the context of ATR and Nyau culture, where people fear ancestral spirits, the message of Romans 8 offers assurance and hope in God.[27]

24 percent of the 116 delegates using Romans 7–8 preached using 8:1–17 about life in Christ/the Holy Spirit:

- Assurance of salvation.[28]

- If a person is guided by the Holy Spirit he is a man of God.[29]

- Distinguishing characteristics of a true Christian.[30]

- Fear not, we received a freedom-spirit to communicate with our father above.[31]

9 percent preached using 8:12–17 about being children of God, though 'adoption' was never mentioned as a category (discussed below):

- Who are led by the spirit of God are children of God.[32]

---

26.   Interview Pastor P2
27.   Interview Pastor P4
28.   Delegate D104 on 8:12–16 (Unknown denomination; town)
29.   Delegate D37 on 8:12–16 (Assemblies of God; village)
30.   Delegate L58 on 8:9–17 (Church of Central Africa, Presbyterian; town)
31.   Delegate L36 on 8:12 (Assemblies of God; trading-centre)
32.   Delegate D20 on 8:14 (Victory Assemblies of God; village)

- Since we are God's children, we must do God's will.[33]

16 percent preached using 8:31–39 about endurance through difficulties, and assurance that nothing can separate the Christian from God's love:

- Trouble cannot separate a man from God.[34]

- We have to endure in difficulties.[35]

Surprisingly, Romans 8:18–30 was a little-used paragraph. It celebrates that present suffering will be replaced by future glory. Contextually interpreted, this is an unused source of potential comfort for those facing suffering or loss.

ii)   Between Horizons

In Paul's context, he was writing to Roman house churches that likely contained slaves. Human existence is never totally secure, but for slaves and those on the margins of society, life was particularly precarious. In 8:15, the phrase translated "spirit of adoption" (πνεῦμα υἱοθεσία) means the exact opposite of the "spirit of slavery" (BDAG, 1024). Paul is here painting a picture of unimaginable security granted by 'adoption' into God's family.

While Jews did not practice legal adoption, the Greco-Roman practice was that a man could formally confer the legal rights of a birth child to someone. This is Paul's likely use. Bruce (1977, 158) comments:

> An adopted son was a son deliberately chosen by his adoptive father to perpetuate his name and inherit his estate; he was no whit inferior in status to a son born in the ordinary course of nature.

Paul is using the metaphor of Roman adoption to describe a status change from inferior slavery to superior sonship.

For those on the margins of Roman society, there could be no higher status than becoming a child of God. This conferred equality with the emperor, who himself claimed to be the son of a deity (Oakes 2009, 137). For a Roman slave this marks a step-change in status, synonymous with freedom. Female slaves were often acquired as 'exposed' infants after abandonment in a public place to die. Promises of adoption might have been particularly evocative for them.

Malawian preachers did not mentioned adoption by name. To second-horizon ears, familiar with legal adoption, this may seem surprising given

---

33.   Delegate L21 on 8:12–14 (Zambezi Evangelical Church; village)
34.   Delegate D10 on 8:35–36 (Living Waters Church; village)
35.   Delegate L34 on 8:35–36 (Assemblies of God; village)

the number of orphans in Malawi. However, such children are simply incorporated into extended families using non-legal processes, taken in by those able and willing to give care. Mateyu (2012) argues that many African Christians fail to understand adoption as a privilege of salvation because such notions barely exist in their culture. The Malawian concept of extended family and community may thus obscure the richness of Paul's metaphor.

While there is no slavery in contemporary Malawi, there is a system of semi-voluntary patronage. Poor villagers without land or houses may work for others in exchange for food and shelter. In practice, there is little realistic hope of escape. To recognize that God offers them a new status as his child may bring assurance and self-worth. This is potentially an important aspect of salvation for rural Malawians trapped by poverty, sickness and suffering.

The adopted person also becomes heir of an inheritance (v. 17). In ancient Rome, "many urban slaves gained freedom. Only a few were fortunate enough to gain inheritances" (Oakes 2009, 137). Malawians are heirs too, their new status yet remaining incomplete and benefits partial. In the present, they must still cry out in dependence to God as their father (v. 15–16), and walk the road of suffering with Christ (v. 17).

Life beyond death seems implicit in Paul's first-horizon notions of inheritance. Here, there is promise for the Malawian to escape eventually from frustration, death and decay (vv. 19–21). Furthermore, "believers enter into full enjoyment of their υιοθεσία [adoption] only when the time of fulfilment releases them from the earthly body" (BDAG, 1024). Paul promises that the entire person will be redeemed, including the body (vv. 11, 23). Such adoption is therefore both a present reality (vv. 14–16) and a future promise (v. 23).

In Oakes' putative reconstruction of the Roman house churches, the sexually exploited slave girl 'Iris' (2009, 143–149) would also have experienced a moral now-and-not-yet tension. She would have been compelled to perform unrighteous sexual activities without any moral choice by her human owners. Yet she would have heard from Paul's letter that she had already been granted a righteous identity and liberated status through rebirth in Christ, her true owner. Though inescapably alive to sin temporally, she was already dead to sin eternally. Perhaps she coped with this inescapable moral tension by desensitization or compartmentalisation – seeking to "count herself dead to sin but alive to God" (6:11) by doing good whenever she had the freedom, opportunity and control to do so.

Those in Malawi who are crippled by poverty, disability or sickness, sexually exploited or in village prostitution face similar now-and-not-yet tensions. Notions of salvation may be identified primarily with their acute felt needs of physical deliverance from affliction – power for the powerless, food for the hungry, liberty for the bound and justice for the oppressed. Yet the majority will not see appreciable healing of their consequentially damaged bodies, minds and emotions in this life; such healing will only be realised fully in the future kingdom. The quest for relief from material suffering may indeed displace their appreciation of man's deepest need, for spiritual freedom from sin and guilt.

Rural Malawians do need a hope of future glory in their daily lives. Any 'over-realized' eschatology that views this life as the full enjoyment of God's blessings is wholly inadequate. In a low-literacy culture, singing, listening to Scripture and prayer may help practically to establish and maintain such future hope. Meanwhile, God is involved in their struggles here and now, through the Spirit (v. 26).

In 5:3–5, Paul tells the Roman house churches that suffering produces perseverance, which produces character, which produces hope. In a Contextual Bible Study, the Malawian participants in their natural third-horizon focussed their discussions upon the benefits of developing good character through perseverance as a consequence of unavoidable suffering. Their desire was for the suffering to be "used well", creating hope.[36] As a second-horizon observer, this seemed a rich spirituality unfamiliar to many in the West, where intuitively, suffering is often viewed as inconvenient and of no lasting value.

e) Compassion amidst Poverty (12:3–21)

i) Existing Use

Poverty creates vulnerability. In Romans chapters 12–16, Paul describes how the new status of son and heir should look in practice. Having already discussed 12:1–2 (section 4.4), we now consider verses 3–21. These verses were cited by 30 percent of the 115 delegates that preached from Romans 12–16.

---

36.   Deacons' Contextual Bible Study, Likuni.

The paragraph 12:3–21 was used to teach compassionate Christian living: humility (v. 3), using gifts (vv. 4–8), love and sincerity towards others (vv. 9–12), generosity (v. 13), and not holding grudges (vv. 14–21):

- Associate with the humble. Do not be wise in your own opinion.[37]
- One body has many parts.[38]
- The need for love and prayerful life.[39]
- Giving and blessing.[40]
- Grudges should be put away for us to develop love.[41]
- If your enemy is hungry feed him.[42]

The topics preached indicate these verses are being applied thoroughly into Malawian life.

ii)   Between Horizons

Grieb (2002, 119–120) reads 12:3–21 from the second-horizon as a set of general illustrative recommendations from Paul about how to "be transformed by the renewing of your mind" (v. 2). In contrast, Oakes (2009, 98), seeking to reconstruct the first-horizon, reads them as direct practical instruction from Paul to an impoverished, socially-diverse house church – a 'how to' manual for living out their new status as sons and heirs with equality and compassion. This reading seems closer to the Malawian third-horizon for two reasons: first, because it is specific and directive as might be expected of Malawian preachers; second, because the social status and problems of both the Roman and Malawian audiences have parallels.

In verse 3, Paul argues against anyone considering themself more important in the church. Oakes (2009, 101) suggests the putative Roman craft workers may have sought honour and patronage through their craft guilds. Some church members may have believed they were superior, based on employment, education, gender or wealth. The preposition γάρ links verse 3 to verses 4–5, which explains that church members are inter-dependent,

---

37. Delegate L81 on 12:3 (United Church of God's Conquerors; town)
38. Delegate D52 on 12:4 (Living Waters Church; trading-centre)
39. Delegate D55 on 12:9–21 (Church of Central Africa, Presbyterian; town)
40. Delegate L38 on 12:13–14 (Church of Christ; village)
41. Delegate L7 on 12:7–21 (Good News Revival Church; town)
42. Delegate D20 on 12:20 (Victory Assemblies of God; village)

not independent – working together like different parts of a body, not as competitors.

How might these verses sound to rural Malawian ears? A number of problems in the Malawian church result from bad attitudes and behaviours by both leaders and/or members (section 3.3d). Gifts (vv. 6–8) are given to equip the whole body.

- Gifts of "serving", "teaching" and "leading" (vv. 7–8). Delegates highlighted that many people enter ministry from wrong motives – hungry for power, authority, popularity or money – and lack integrity. Yet Paul says the leaders themselves should perform these gifts "diligently" (v. 8).

- Gifts of "sharing" and "showing mercy" (v. 8). Although church members may differ widely in their income, "sharing" may prove acutely burdensome economically, since even the wealthiest are relatively poor. Yet Paul says these gifts should be exercised "simply" and "cheerfully" (v. 8).

"Sharing" includes "practicing hospitality" (v. 13). The obligation in ancient societies to provide hospitality to strangers has been largely lost in the modern West. But in Malawi this might be heard as encouragement to continue giving food and shelter to poorer members of the extended family, orphans, disabled, landless families and migrant workers. In villages this responsibility might fall on those with the largest farms.[43] Yet everyone might contribute gifts like maize seed, or give assistance after childbirth, in sickness or with elderly – not necessarily money. In the West, many of these aspects would be provided through the safety net of government benefits.

Some may seek to take financial advantage of the poor. Oakes (2009, 118) suggests in the Roman world, to curse someone (v. 14) was akin to taking revenge. In the contemporary West, verbal abuse is viewed far less seriously than physical assault. But in Africa, cursing is taken very seriously. Mbiti (1989, 151) writes: "The curse is something greatly feared in many societies, and a powerful curse is believed to bring death to the person concerned." This verse might restrain those facing economic ruin through the greed and exploitation of others. People are instructed to come alongside one another and agree (vv. 15–16), not to take retribution (vv. 17–21). The goal is to elevate

---

43.   Interview Pastor P2

the poor to your own level, not to maintain personal position in the hierarchy of Malawian society (v. 16).

In conclusion, this section indicates that the churches of first-horizon ancient Rome and the natural third-horizon of contemporary Malawi may have similar social dynamics in relation to poverty and compassion. The increasing introduction of Western culture, values and concepts of wealth into rural Malawian communities, and the potential influence of interpreters trained in the second-horizon, risks hindering Malawian preachers and congregations from developing their own contextual understandings of the text.

5.4 Summary

This chapter identifies paragraphs of Romans that are used for preaching in provincial-rural Malawi, though far less frequently than the popular individual/pairs of verses discussed in chapter 4. The chapter then offers some contextual readings of paragraphs of Romans in the third-horizon which relate to the problems experienced by church leaders.

These studies conclude:

a) Lively faith is important to prevent backsliding into traditional religion and practice which is so deeply ingrained in the Malawian worldview. Contextually, faith is expressed in action and best illustrated through concrete positive examples like Abraham.

b) Initiation rituals are important in Malawian life. Circumcision is a socio-religious practice observed by Islam and ATR. There is pressure to allow this practice into churches, but it risks introducing syncretic practices and works/righteousness theologies into the church. The alternative is shown to be lively faith and godly living.

c) Christian marriage is challenged by the traditional Malawian acceptance of male polygamy, adultery and negative attitudes towards women. By radical rereading of Paul's marriage illustration, a narrative tool was created to oppose immorality and promote the values of Christian marriage.

d) When rural Malawian Christians face suffering, sickness or death they often revert to traditional medicine and beliefs. At such times, they especially need assurance through knowing their new status as child of God and future inheritance in Christ.

e) The most vulnerable need compassion. Malawian churches should lead the way in helping the most vulnerable by sharing meagre resources and hospitality. The financial burden should fall on everyone, according to their means, recognizing this will be costly for all, and not to retaliate if some take advantage of them.

6

Conclusion

This study uses a three-horizon contextual approach to interpret the Letter to the Romans in the context of contemporary provincial-rural Malawi. To achieve this, it seeks to satisfy three aspects of Biblical interpretation:

- To read Romans in the author's context, reconstructing as far as possible the meaning conveyed to the original audience in their world.

- To respect particularity of meaning in verses/paragraphs, discerning what key words signify in their literary, historical and socio-cultural contexts.

- To link the original context to current contexts, considering how the natural third-horizon of provincial-rural Malawi resembles or differs from the original first-horizon and mediating second-horizons.

Three research questions have driven this study:

1. What are the socio-cultural and pastoral issues experienced by church leaders in provincial-rural Malawi?

2. How is the letter to the Romans currently used and interpreted in provincial-rural Malawi?

3. How might Romans be used, in the context of provincial-rural Malawi, to address these socio-cultural and pastoral issues?

Question 1 has resulted in a picture of an under-trained local church leadership set against a catalogue of socio-cultural and pastoral problems which impact Christian ministry. This perspective of life and ministry was adopted as a model to represent the third-horizon context of provincial-rural Malawi.

The socio-cultural and pastoral problems included:

- Muslim activities, especially festivals, rituals and initiations like circumcision, which enter the church and cause confusion.
- African traditional religion and culture, including magic, witchcraft and traditional medicine, which cause backsliding and fear.
- Social transition rites, funerals and Nyau culture.
- Sexual and marital issues like polygamy, infidelity and oppression of women.
- Bad behaviour like drunkenness, disunity, division, greed, gossiping and lying.

Traditional practices were expressed most freely in villages where church leaders with the lowest levels of training and experience often served. Lack of training was especially acute among non-pastors.

Question 2 has shown that trained and experienced pastors were the church leaders most likely to use Romans in preaching. Many church leaders quoted one of five highly popular verses/verse pairs in their preaching (1:16–17; 3:23; 6:23; 10:9–10 and 12:1–2), typically as part of a simple gospel presentation. The main driving force behind this preaching was to make new converts and promote Christianity against traditional religion. Sermons often used prominent theological words in or near these verses, like power, salvation, redemption, freedom and sacrifice. Such words were usually interpreted literally and without contextualisation.

Complete paragraphs were less commonly used in preaching. These sermons were generally topical, inductive responses to felt needs. Many preachers understood that Paul used allegories – "circumcision of the heart" (2:29), "baptism" (6:4), "marriage" (7:1–6) – but some applied such images literally. Preachers sometimes included contextualisation, for example Abraham as an exemplary ancestor as well as a pattern for active faith that "works". Nevertheless, many Malawians found Romans too difficult, and chose to use other texts instead, especially narratives.

Question 3 has demonstrated there is potential to create rich contextual readings of Romans that will engage the problems of Malawian life. Social aspects of salvation like covenant faithfulness (which offers hope and restoration) and impartial justice (which rectifies wrongs) show that God powerfully will meet the felt-needs of the poor, and may be trusted. He is seen to offer them more than judicial forgiveness and freedom from guilt.

Interpretation in the natural third-horizon of Malawi needs to break free from the presuppositions of the Western second-horizon.

Contextualization relates Christian living to Malawian life. For example:

- faith sealed through godly actions, not rituals

- total sacrifice of life, not token sacrifices at festivals

- security and future hope as a child of God

- holiness and self-worth for the sexually exploited and abused

- compassion and protection for the destitute and landless

In the introduction to this work, Ukpong (2002, 17) said: "African readings are existential and pragmatic in nature, and contextual in approach . . . and lay no claim to a universal perspective." Does this study support his assertion? Yes, partially:

- Many interpretations of Romans *are* indeed "existential and pragmatic", engaging with issues affecting Christian devotion, practical living and human survival.

- Most interpretations were *not* "contextual in approach", but were often either literal explanations of theological key words, or interpretations at least partially originating in second-horizon Western contexts.

- Some preachers did use contextual imagery such as ancestors, and Biblical imagery of contextual relevance like slavery and sonship. However, there was "no . . . universal perspective". Rather, there was a range of interpretations, literal and allegorical. Interpretation in provincial-rural Malawi is thus driven by local concerns in the natural third-horizon, with some interference by second-horizon Western influences such as previous training.

Bibliography

Aguilar, L. B. 2009. 'Inculturating Nyau: Nyau Masks in a Christian Paradigm' in *Material Religion* Vol. 5, No.1: 105–107

Appiah-Kubi, K. 1987. 'Christology', 69–81 in J Parratt (ed.) *A Reader in African Christian Theology*. London: SPCK.

Barratt, D. B. 1968. *Schism and Renewal in Africa: An Analysis of Six Thousand Contemporary Religious Movements*. London: OUP.

BDAG, Bauer W. *et al.* (eds). 2000. *Greek-English Lexicon of the New Testament and other Early Christian Literature 3ʳᵈ Edition*. Chicago: University of Chicago Press.

Bediako, K. 1995. *Christianity in Africa: the Renewal of a Non-Western Religion*. Edinburgh: Edinburgh University Press.

Bird, M. F. & Sprinkle, P. M. (eds). 2009. *The Faith of Jesus Christ: Exegetical, Biblical and Theological Studies*. Milton Keynes: Paternoster.

Bruce, F. F. 1977. *Romans: An Introduction and Commentary* (TNTC). Leicester: InterVarsity Press.

Bujo, B. 1992. *African Theology in its Social Context*. Maryknoll: Orbis.

Carson, D. A. 1984. 'A Sketch of the Factors Determining Current Hermeneutical Debate in Cross-Cultural Contexts', 11–29 in D. A. Carson (ed.) *Biblical Interpretation and the Church: Text and Context*. Exeter: Paternoster.

Chakanza, J. C. 1982. 'Towards an Interpretation of Independent Churches in Malawi' in *Africa Theological Journal* Vol.11, No.2, 133–142.

Dada, A.O. 2010. 'Repositioning Contextual Biblical Hermeneutics in Africa towards Holistic Empowerment' in *Black Theology: An International Journal* Vol. 8, No.2, 160–174.

Das, A.A. 2007. *Solving the Romans Debate*. Minneapolis: Fortress Press.

Dicks, I.D. 2012. *An African Worldview. The Muslim Amacinga Yawo of Southern Malawi*, Kachere Monograph No. 32. Zomba, Malawi: Kachere Series.

Donfried, K. P. 1991. 'False presuppositions in the Study of Romans' 102–125 in K. P. Donfried (ed.) *The Romans Debate*. Peabody: Hendrickson.

Dunn, J. D. G. 1988a. *Romans 1–8* (WBC). Nashville: Thomas Nelson.

———. 1988b. *Romans 9–16* (WBC). Nashville: Thomas Nelson.

———. 2006. *The Parting of the Ways: Between Christianity and Judaism and their Significance for the Character of Christianity*, 2ⁿᵈ Edition. London: SCM Press.

EDNT, Balz, H. & Schneider, G. (eds). 1993. *Exegetical Dictionary of the New Testament* (3 volumes). Grand Rapids: Eerdmans.

Esler, P. F. 2003. *Conflict and Identity in Romans: the Social Setting of Paul's Letter*. Minneapolis: Augsburg Fortress. Available (limited page preview) from: http://

books.google.co.uk/books?id=QB9QPS4NA50C&printsec=frontcover&dq=
esler+conflict&hl=en&ei=VeMATaWiDI-GhQeZtsTtBw&sa=X&oi=book_
result&ct=result&resnum=1&ved=0CCYQ6AEwAA#v=onepage&q&f=false
(accessed 11 Sep 12)

Fee, G. D. & Stuart, D. 2003. *How to Read the Bible for All It's Worth*, 3rd Edition.
Grand Rapids: Zondervan.

Fiedler, R. N. 2007. *Coming of Age: A Christianized Initiation among Women in
Southern Malawi*, Kachere Text No. 25. Zomba, Malawi: Kachere Series.

Gehman, R. J. 1989. *African Traditional Religion in Biblical Perspective*. Kijabe,
Kenya: Kesho Publications.

Grieb, A. K. 2002. *The Story of Romans: A Narrative Defence of God's Righteousness*.
Louisville: Westminster John Knox Press.

Ijalasi, C. 2012. *90% untrained* [Interview] by email with Jonathan Groves. 11
January 2012.

Jeffers, J. S. 2002. 'Slaves of God: The Impact of the Cult of the Roman Emperor
on Paul's Use of the Language of Power Relations' *Fides et Historia* Vol. 34,
No.1, 123–139.

Jewett, R. 2007. *Romans: A Commentary*. Minneapolis: Fortress Press.

Kalilombe, P. A. 1999. *Doing Theology at the Grassroots: Theological Essays from
Malawi*. Kachere Book No. 7. Gweru, Zimbabwe: Mambo Press.

Kanyoro, M. 1999. 'Reading the Bible from an African Perspective' in *Ecumenical
Review* Vol.51, No.1, 18–24.

Kanyumi, D. 2011. *A glimpse of what God is doing here in Malawi: Zambesi Mission
News – Sept 2011*. Available from: http://www.zambesimission.org/pages/
news11-9.html (accessed 02 Mar 12)

Kärkkäinen, V–M. 2003. *Christology: A Global Introduction*. Grand Rapids: Baker.

Lausanne. 1974. *Lausanne Covenant*. Available from http://www.lausanne.org/en/
documents/lausanne-covenant.html (accessed 28 Feb 12)

LeMarquand, G. 2005. 'African Biblical Interpretation'. 31–34 in K. J. Vanhoozer
(ed.) *Dictionary for Theological Interpretation of the Bible*. Grand Rapids: Baker.

Longwe, M. 2007. *Growing Up: A Chewa Girls' Initiation*. Kachere Thesis No. 15.
Zomba, Malawi: Kachere Series.

Malawi Project. 2012. *Trading Centres*. Available from: http://www.malawiproject.
org/about-malawi/trading-centers (accessed 10 Sep 12)

Mandryk, J. 2010. *Operation World,* 7th Edition. Colorado Springs: Biblica.

Manglos, N. D. 2010. 'Born Again in Balaka: Pentecostal Verses Catholic Narratives
of Religious Transformation in Rural Malawi' in *Sociology of Religion* Vol.71,
No.4, 409–431.

———. 2011. 'Brokerage in the Sacred Sphere: Religious Leaders as Community
Problem Solvers in Rural Malawi' in *Sociological Forum* Vol.26, No.2, 334–355.

Mateyu, S. 2011. [Interview] by email with Jonathan Groves. 13 January 2011.

————. 2012. *The Doctrine of Adoption: Its Meaning and Relevance from an African Perspective.* Saarbrücken: Lambert Academic Publishing.

Mbiti, J. S. 1975. *An Introduction to African Religion.* London: Heinemann.

————. 1986. *Bible and Theology in African Christianity.* Nairobi: Oxford University Press.

————. 1989. *African Religions and Philosophy,* 2nd Edition. Oxford: Heinemann Educational.

Mijoga, H. B. P. 1996. 'Hermeneutics in African Instituted Churches in Malawi' in *Missionalia* Vol. 24, No. 3, 358–371.

————. 2000. *Separate but the Same Gospel: Preaching in African Instituted Churches in Southern Malawi.* Kachere Study No. 2. Blantyre, Malawi: CLAIM.

————. 2003. 'The Old Testament Background of Paul's Phrase "Works of the Law"', in *Malawi Journal of Biblical Studies* Vol. 1, 5–8.

Msiska, S.K. 1996. 'The Certainty of Christianity among the People in the Villages' 69–79 in K. R. Ross (ed.) *Christianity in Malawi: A Source Book.* Kachere Books No. 3. Gweru, Zimbabwe: Mambo Press.

Moo, D. 1991. *Romans 1–8* (Wycliffe Exegetical Commentary). Chicago: Moody Press.

Morris, L. 1988. *The Epistle to the Romans* (PNTC). Leicester: Apollos.

Naidoo, M. 2010. 'Ministerial Training: The Need for Pedagogies of Formation and of Contextualisation in Theological Education' in *Missionalia* Vol. 38, No. 3, 347–368.

Nyende, P. 2009. 'Ethnic Studies: An Urgent Need in Theological Education in Africa' in *International Review of Mission* Vol. 98, No. 1, 132–146.

Oakes, P. 2009. *Reading Romans in Pompeii: Paul's Letter at Ground Level.* London: SPCK.

Padilla, C. R. 1981. 'The Interpreted Word: Reflections on Contextual Hermeneutics' in *Themelios* Vol. 7, No. 1, 18–23.

Riches, J. 2010. *What is Contextual Bible Study? A Practical Guide with Group Studies for Advent and Lent.* London: SPCK.

Ross, K. R. 1995a. 'Contemporary Preaching in Mainstream Christian Churches in Malawi: A Survey and Analysis', 81–106 in K. R. Ross (ed.) *Gospel Ferment in Malawi: Theological Essays.* Gweru, Zimbabwe: Mambo Press.

Ross, K. R. (ed.). 1995b. *Church, University and Theological Education in Malawi,* Kachere Text. Zomba: University of Malawi.

Sanneh, L. 1990. *Translating the Message: The Missionary Impact on Culture.* Maryknoll: Orbis.

Schreiner, T. R. 1998. *Romans* (BECNT). Grand Rapids: Baker Academic.

Sear, R. 2008. 'Kin and Child Survival in Rural Malawi: Are Matrilineal Kin always Beneficial in a Matrilineal Society?' in *Human Nature* Vol. 19, 277–293.

Smith, David W. "The letter to the Romans and mission in a troubled, urban world." In *The Kindness of God. Christian Witness in our Troubled World*, edited by David W. Smith, 120–150. Nottingham: IVP, 2013.

SIM. 2011. *Pastors' Book Set – Malawi*. Available from: http://www.sim.org/index.php/project/96558 (accessed 29 Feb 12)

Stinton, D. 2004. *Jesus of Africa: Voices of Contemporary Christology*. Maryknoll: Orbis.

Thiselton, A. C. 1980. *The Two Horizons: New Testament Hermeneutics and Philosophical Description*. Grand Rapids: Eerdmans.

UNDP Malawi, 2012. *United Nations Development Programme Malawi: Millenium Development Goals in Malawi*. Available from: http://www.undp.org.mw/index.php?option=com_content&view=article&id=465&Itemid=187 (accessed 18 Aug 12)

USCWM. 2007. Roberta Winter Institute website. Available from: http://www.uscwm.org/rwi/compare_projects.html (accessed 29 Feb 12)

Ukpong, J. S. 2000. 'Developments in Biblical Interpretation in Africa: Historical and Hermeneutical Directions' 11–27 in GO West & M. W. Dube (eds) *The Bible in Africa: Transactions, Trajectories, and Trends*. Leiden: Brill Academic.

———. 2002. 'Inculturation Hermeneutics: An African Approach to Biblical Interpretation' 17–32 in W. Dietrich & U. Luz (eds) *The Bible in a World Context: an Experiment in Contextual Hermeneutics*. Grand Rapids: Eerdmans.

VanBreugel, J. W. M. 2001. *Chewa Traditional Religion*, Kachere Monograph No. 13. Blantyre, Malawi: CLAIM.

Van der Meer, E. 2010. 'Strategic Level Spiritual Warfare and Mission in Africa' in *Evangelical Review of Theology* Vol. 34, No. 2, 155–166.

———. 2011, 'The Problem of Witchcraft in Malawi' in *Evangelical Missions Quarterly* Vol. 47, No. 1, 78–85.

Vanhoozer, K. J. 1998. *Is There a Meaning in this Text? The Bible, the Reader and the Morality of Literary Knowledge*. Leicester: Apollos.

Waweru, H. M. 2006. 'Reading the Bible Contrapuntally: A Theory and Methodology for a Contextual Bible Interpretation in Africa' in *Swedish Missiological Themes* Vol. 94, No. 3, 333–348.

Wendland, E. R. & Hachibamba, S. 2007. *Galu Wamkota: Missiological Reflections from South-Central Africa*, Kachere Monograph No. 25. Zomba, Malawi: Kachere Series.

Wendland, E. R. 1998. *Buku Loyera: An Introduction to the New Chichewa Translation*, Kachere Monograph No. 6. Blantyre, Malawi: CLAIM.

———. 2000, *Preaching that Grabs the Heart: A Rhetorical-Stylistic Study of the Chewa Revival Sermons of Shadrack Warne*, Kachere Monograph No. 11. Blantyre, Malawi: CLAIM.

West, GO. 2008. *Biblical Hermeneutics in Africa*. Available from: http://www.chora-strangers.org/files/chora/west2008_Parratt.pdf (accessed 28 Feb 12)

Witherington, B. 2004. *Paul's Letter to the Romans: A Socio-Rhetorical Commentary*. Grand Rapids: Eerdmans.

Wright, N. T. 1997. *What Saint Paul Really Said*. Grand Rapids: Eerdmans.

———. 2005, *Paul: In Fresh Perspective*. London: SPCK.

Bibles in Chichewa

Buku Lopatulika (1922)

The Bible in Chichewa, published as *Buku Lopatulika ndilo Mau a Mulungu*. Blantyre: Bible Society of Malawi

Buku Loyera (1998)

The Bible with Deuterocanonicals in Chichewa, published as *Buku Loyera*. Blantyre: Bible Society of Malawi

Tables

Table 1 Experience as a pastor: The table shows the number of delegates who are pastors (and as percentage of pastors) or non-pastors at the Liwonde and Mponela conferences. Pastors are subdivided according to the number of years they have served as a pastor. Data based on 179 questionnaires.

Years as Pastor	Total	Liwonde	Mponela
0–2	22 (21%)	10 (20%)	12 (22%)
3–5	33 (31%)	17 (34%)	16 (29%)
6–10	19 (18%)	7 (14%)	12 (22%)
10+	31 (30%)	16 (32%)	15 (27%)
Total Pastors	105 (100%)	50 (100%)	55 (100%)
Non-pastors	74	49	25

Table 2 Size of Congregation: The table shows the number (percentage) of delegates by size of congregation in which they serve at the Liwonde and Mponela conferences. Data based on 177 questionnaires (2 non-respondents at Liwonde).

Size of Congregation	Total	Liwonde	Mponela
0–25	28 (16%)	12 (12%)	16 (20%)
25–100	80 (45%)	48 (49%)	32 (40%)
100–250	32 (18%)	18 (19%)	14 (18%)
250+	37 (21%)	19 (20%)	18 (23%)
Total	177 (100%)	97 (100%)	80 (100%)

Table 3 Size of Congregation: The table shows the total number of delegates by size of congregation in which they serve cross-tabulated against the location of the church. Data based on 177 questionnaires (2 non-respondents).

Size of Congregation	All locations	In Town	In Village	Other
0–25	28 (16%)	6 (9%)	21 (23%)	1
25–100	80 (45%)	23 (33%)	52 (57%)	5
100–250	32 (18%)	16 (23%)	10 (11%)	6
250+	37 (21%)	24 (35%)	8 (9%)	5
Total	177 (100%)	69 (100%)	91 (100%)	17

Table 4 Experience as a pastor: The table shows the number of delegates who are pastors (and as percentage of pastors) or non-pastors cross-tabulated against the location of the church. Pastors are subdivided according to the number of years they have served as a pastor. Data based on 178 questionnaires (1 non-respondent).

Years as Pastor	All locations	In Town	In Village	Other
0–2	22 (21%)	4 (11%)	16 (29%)	2
3–5	33 (31%)	12 (32%)	20 (36%)	1
6–10	19 (18%)	4 (11%)	9 (16%)	6
10+	31 (30%)	18 (47%)	11 (20%)	2
Total Pastors	105 (100%)	38 (100%)	56 (100%)	11
Non-pastors	73	32	35	6

Table 5 Denominational affiliation of delegates at the Liwonde and Mponela conferences

Denomination	Total	Liwonde	Mponela
African Abraham Church International	3	–	3
African Church	1	–	1
Anglican Church	1	–	1
Antioch International Church	2	2	–
Apostolic Faith Mission	2	1	1
Assemblies Movement Church	1	–	1
Assemblies of God	44	12	32
Baptist	7	5	2
Calvary Family Church	4	3	1
Charismatic Redeemed Ministries International	5	4	1
Christ Citadel International	3	3	–
Church of Central Africa, Presbyterian	24	20	4
Church of Christ	1	1	–
Church on the Rock	1	1	–
Eleventh Hour Labourers Ministry	1	–	1
Evangelical (undefined)	1	1	–
Evangelical Baptist Church of Malawi	7	7	–
Fountain Waters of Life Church	1	–	1
Good News Revival Church	8	8	–
Good Samaritan Church	4	4	–
Kingdom Gospel Church	1	1	–
Living Waters Church	21	5	16
Malawi Council of Churches	1	1	–
Miracle Church of God	1	–	1
New Last Truth of God Church	6	–	6
Pentecostal Church	3	–	3
Pentecostal Holiness Association Church	3	2	1
Roman Catholic Church	1	1	–
Seventh Day Adventist	1	1	–

United Church of God's Conquerors	3	3	–
Victory Assemblies of God	1	–	1
Victory Pentecostal Church	3	3	–
Zambezi Evangelical Church	10	8	2
Unknown	3	2	1
TOTAL	**179**	**99**	**80**

Table 6 Aspects of Malawian life and culture that cause difficulties in the churches of conference delegates. Data shows the number of reports of an issue from the 99 and 80 delegates returning basic questionnaires at the Liwonde and Mponela conferences. In Liwonde, the issue "Initiation Ceremonies" may include undifferentiated Muslim and traditional cultural practices, or a fusion of the two, as discussed in the text.

Group	Issue	Liwonde	Mponela
	Circumcision	20	1
	Other Muslim practices	13	3
Muslim Culture & Practices		**33 (14%)**	**4 (2%)**
	Initiation ceremonies	28	2
	Traditional religion & practice	31	22
	Nyau culture / *Gule wamkulu*	5	38
	Other traditional dances	3	2
	Magic / Witchcraft	23	14
	Diviners / Traditional medicine	15	15
	Funeral rituals / Ancestors	10	2
Traditional Culture & Practices		**115 (50%)**	**95 (56%)**
	Polygamy	19	18
	Marriage problems / Divorce	8	5
	Premarital sex / Marriage customs	5	4
	Homosexuality	–	5
	Prostitution	–	4
Sex & Marriage Customs		**32 (14%)**	**36 (21%)**
	Problems with church members	10	10
	Drunkenness	10	6
	Problems with church leaders	6	3
	Dress-code differences	1	3
	Politics, power and corruption	2	1
	Secularism	–	3
	Smoking / Tobacco / Drugs	2	1
	Inheritance of property	1	1
Other Attitudes & Behaviours		**32 (14%)**	**28 (17%)**

	Lack of education	10	2
	Poverty	6	4
	Economic / Financial problems	2	–
	Sickness	–	1
Poverty & Deprivation		**18 (8%)**	**7 (4%)**
TOTAL		**231**	**169**

Table 7 Use of Romans in preaching cross-tabulated against church leadership role and level of ministry experience if a Pastor: The table shows the number of delegates (percentage of those with that role and experience level) that had used at least one verse from a section of Romans in their preaching over recent years. The results are based on 179 basic questionnaires returned by 55 Inexperienced Pastors (0–5 years of service), 50 Experienced Pastors (6+ years), and 74 Non-pastors, from Liwonde and Mponela combined.

Section of Romans	Section has been used by any delegate	Section has been used by Inexperienced Pastor	Section has been used by Experienced Pastor	Section has been used by Non-pastor
chapter 1	110 (61%)	37 (67%)	42 (84%)	31 (42%)
chapter 2–3	102 (57%)	33 (60%)	39 (78%)	30 (41%)
chapter 4–6	114 (64%)	38 (69%)	42 (84%)	34 (46%)
chapter 7–8	118 (66%)	40 (73%)	41 (82%)	37 (50%)
chapter 9–11	96 (54%)	36 (65%)	34 (68%)	26 (35%)
chapter 12–16	111 (62%)	36 (65%)	38 (76%)	37 (50%)
Total delegates	**179 (100%)**	**55 (100%)**	**50 (100%)**	**74 (100%)**

Table 8 Use of Romans in preaching by leadership role cross-tabulated against the level of previous training of the preacher. The table shows the number (percentage) of Pastors and Non-pastors that had used at least one verse from a section of Romans in their preaching over recent years. The results are based on 179 basic questionnaires returned by 74 Trained and 31 Untrained Pastors, and by 19 Trained and 55 Untrained Non-pastors, from Liwonde and Mponela combined.

Section of Romans	Role of delegate	Section has been used by any delegate	Section has been used by Trained delegate	Section has been used by Untrained delegate
chapter 1	Pastor	79 (75%)	61 (82%)	18 (58%)
	Non-pastor	31 (42%)	14 (74%)	17 (31%)
chapter 2–3	Pastor	72 (69%)	53 (72%)	19 (61%)
	Non-pastor	30 (41%)	11 (58%)	19 (35%)
chapter 4–6	Pastor	80 (76%)	59 (80%)	21 (68%)
	Non-pastor	34 (46%)	11 (58%)	23 (42%)
chapter 7–8	Pastor	81 (77%)	61 (82%)	20 (61%)
	Non-pastor	37 (50%)	11 (58%)	26 (47%)
chapter 9–11	Pastor	70 (67%)	52 (70%)	18 (58%)
	Non-pastor	26 (34%)	7 (37%)	19 (33%)
chapter 12–16	Pastor	74 (70%)	61 (82%)	13 (42%)
	Non-pastor	37 (50%)	12 (63%)	25 (45%)
Total delegates	**Pastor**	**105 (100%)**	**74 (100%)**	**31 (100%)**
	Non-pastor	**74 (100%)**	**19 (100%)**	**55 (100%)**

Table 9 Most-used paragraphs in preaching from the Letter to the Romans. The table shows groups of at least six verses for which ten or more delegates (over 6 percent of total) had preached from each verse in the group, based on the data in figures 2–6. The stated subject is based on a second–horizon commentary source (Morris, 1988).

Most-used Paragraphs	
Verses	**Subject**
1:8–15	Paul's prayer
2:2–9	Judging, repentance and judgement [Jews]
4:1–8	God's way is grace [Abraham]
6:1–15	Sin so that grace may abound?
8:1–17	Flesh and spirit; Family of God
8:31–39	Christian's triumph song
10:1–15	Two ways of righteousness
12:1–21	Christian attitude to God and others

Table 10 Least-used paragraphs in preaching from the Letter to the Romans. The table shows groups of at least six consecutive verses for which six or fewer delegates (over 0–3 percent of total) had preached from each verse in the group, based on the data in figures 2–6. The stated subject is based on a second-horizon commentary source (Morris, 1988).

Least-used Paragraphs	
Verses	**Subject**
3:1–8	God's faithfulness [Jews]; Objections
5:12–21	Solidarity in Adam and Christ
8:18, 20–30	Glorious future; Spirit's intercession; Purpose of God
9:1–13	Tragedy of Israel; Election
9:16–33	God's wrath and mercy
11:11–36	Restoration and conversion of Israel
14:1–15:13	Liberty; Peace and love; Christian unity
15:14–16:27	Paul's ministry and greetings

Figures

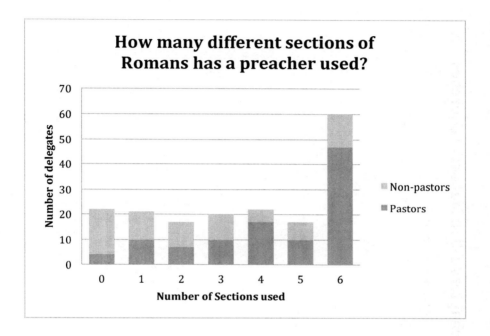

Figure 1 Graph to show the number of different sections of Romans that a provincial-rural church leader has used in their preaching:
The 16 chapters of Romans were nominally divided into six sections: chapter 1, chapter 2–3, chapter 4–6, chapter 7–8, chapter 9–11 and chapter 12–16. The data shows the number of pastors and non-pastors that had used at least one verse from the indicated number of different sections of Romans, from zero up to the maximum of six sections. The results were derived from the basic questionnaires returned by 105 pastors and 74 non-pastors. There was no appreciable difference between the outcomes from Liwonde and Mponela, and the data from both conference locations has been combined. On average, a pastor had preached from 4.3 different sections of Romans, while a non-pastor from 2.6 different sections.

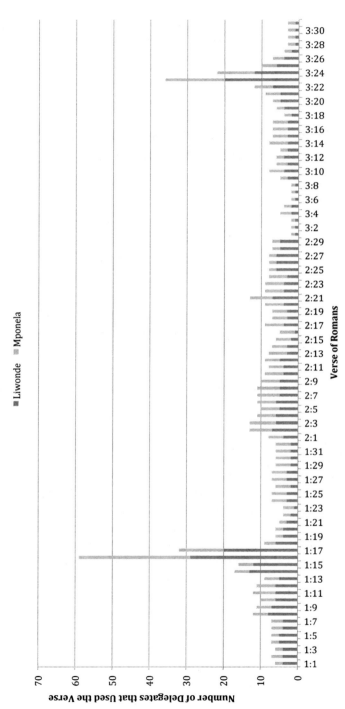

Figure 2 Graph showing the number of church leaders at Liwonde and Mponela that declared they had used verses from Romans chapters 1–3 in their preaching over recent years. The results are derived from all 179 returned questionnaires (99 from Liwonde and 80 from Mponela).

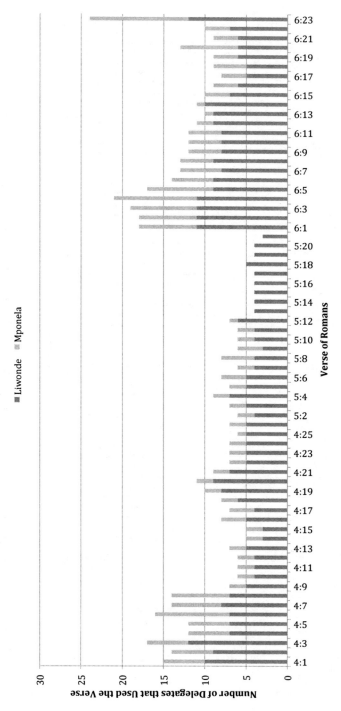

Figure 3 Graph showing the number of church leaders at Liwonde and Mponela that declared they had used verses from Romans chapters 4–6 in their preaching over recent years. The results are derived from all 179 returned questionnaires (99 from Liwonde and 80 from Mponela).

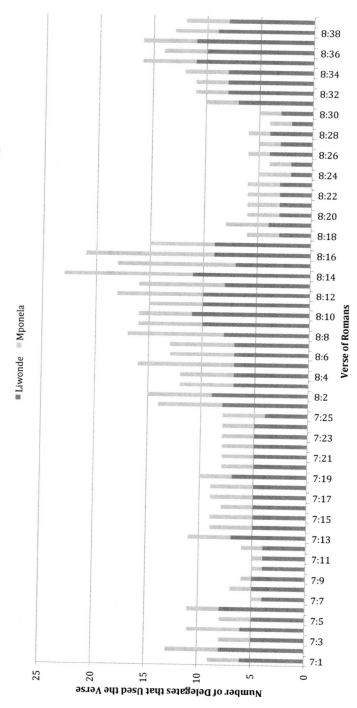

Figure 4 Graph showing the number of church leaders at Liwonde and Mponela that declared they had used verses from Romans chapters 7–8 in their preaching over recent years. The results are derived from all 179 returned questionnaires (99 from Liwonde and 80 from Mponela).

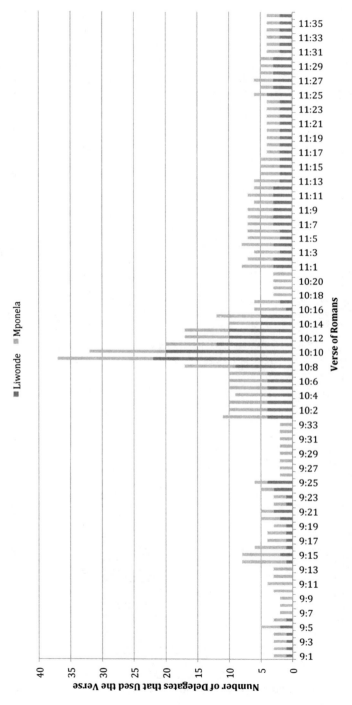

Figure 5 Graph showing the number of church leaders at Liwonde and Mponela that declared they had used verses from Romans chapters 9–11 in their preaching over recent years. The results are derived from all 179 returned questionnaires (99 from Liwonde and 80 from Mponela).

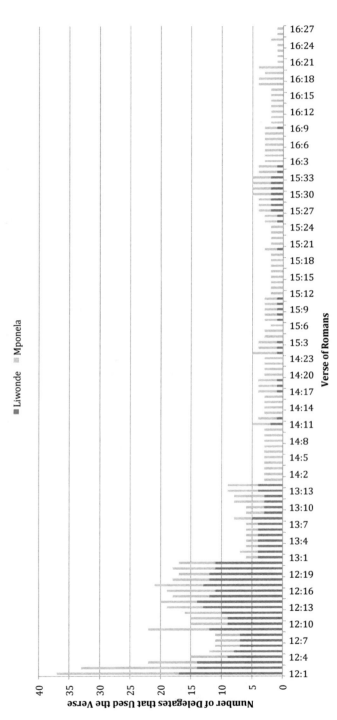

Figure 6 Graph showing the number of church leaders at Liwonde and Mponela that declared they had used verses from Romans chapters 12–16 in their preaching over recent years. The results are derived from all 179 returned questionnaires (99 from Liwonde and 80 from Mponela).

Basic Questionnaire

This questionnaire is a part of my research for a Master of Theology degree. I am studying the use of Paul's letter to the Romans in the evangelical churches of Malawi. All answers to this questionnaire will remain strictly confidential. Your answers will be anonymous unless you write your name in the final question. Please write in English if possible, but otherwise Chichewa is fine. Many thanks for your help!

1. **How many years have you been a Pastor?** *(please circle one)*

   0–2 years   3–5 years   6–10 years   10+ years   Not a Pastor

2. **Where is your church?** *(please circle one)*

   In a Village   In a City   In a Town   Other _____

3. **How large is your church congregation?** *(please circle one)*

   0–25 people   25–100 people   100–250 people   250+ people

4. **Have you personally attended any courses at a Bible school?**
   (please circle one)

   None   Short Course   Extension Course   Full-time Study

5. **How does your church decide upon the subject of its preaching?**
   (please circle one)

   Programme planned   Chosen   From a Lectionary
   well ahead   week-by-week

6. **Which denomination (if any) is your church a part of?**

   _____

   _____

7. **What aspects of Malawian life and culture cause difficulties in your church?**

_____

_____

_____

8. **Have you preached using Romans chapter 1 in the last few years?**
    Yes/No

    If yes, which verses did you use and what subject did you use them to speak about?

    _____

9. **Have you preached using Romans chapters 2–3 in the last few years?**
    Yes/No

    If yes, which verses did you use and what subject did you use them to speak about?

    _____

10. **Have you preached using Romans chapters 4–6 in the last few years?**
    Yes/No

    If yes, which verses did you use and what subject did you use them to speak about?

    _____

11. **Have you preached using Romans chapters 7–8 in the last few years?**
    Yes/No

    If yes, which verses did you use and what subject did you use them to speak about?

    _____

12. **Have you preached using Romans chapters 9–11 in the last few years?** *Yes/No*

    If yes, which verses did you use and what subject did you use them to speak about?

    _____

13. **Have you preached using Romans chapters 12–16 in the last few years?** *Yes/No*

    If yes, which verses did you use and what subject did you use them to speak about?

    _____

14. **In what ways is the Letter to the Romans relevant to the Malawian church today?**

    _____

    _____

    _____

15. **Are you willing to discuss Romans with me in more detail for 15–20min?** *Yes/No*

    If yes, please speak to me during the conference

16. **(Optional) What is your name?** _____

Thank you very much for your help!

Supplementary Questionnaire & Interview Sheet

Issues in Malawian Life and Culture

1. What aspects of Malawian life and culture cause difficulties in your church?

    - Please tell me more about each area

Use of the Letter to the Romans

2. How is Romans used in the Malawian church? Which parts are most used and why?

3. Are some parts of Romans used only rarely? Why not more often?

Issues in Life and Romans

4. Which of the life difficulties you have mentioned (above) does Romans speak into? How?

5. Conversely, which parts of Romans do not connect with Malawian Christians? Why not?

Romans in Specific Areas of Life

6. **Does Romans have anything to say to the Malawian church about:**
    - The story of salvation
    - Christianity as an outside religion to Africa
    - Traditional religion or witchcraft
    - Poverty, health or education
    - Ethnic diversity
    - Politics, power and corruption

7. **Do people turn (back) to traditional religion if they have difficulties?**
    - How do pastors respond to this? Could use of Romans help persuade them not to?

8. **Is ethnic diversity and tribalism an issue in the Malawian church?**

- How do pastors deal with it? Could any part of Romans help them with this?

How to Interpret Romans

9. **How do you 'read' Romans? (What is your preferred approach to it as literature?)**
    - Is it doctrinal statements, theological story, practical instruction, something else?

10. **How could pastors be helped to better understand and use Romans? Training?**

Appendix C

Chichewa Bible Translations

a) Introduction

Effective vernacular translations help to make the Christian gospel more accessible and its character less foreign (Sanneh 1990, 159). Most importantly, they enable God to speak directly into people's hearts through his Word using their mother tongue (Acts 2:11). Translation is about communication of meaning into a particular culture. Barrett notes: "Vernacular scriptures have far greater power to communicate and create religious dynamic than versions in *lingua francae* . . . The vernacular translation enables the ethnic group concerned to grasp the inner meanings of . . . profound and intricate biblical doctrines" (D. Barrett in Sanneh 1990, 188).

For all except the most highly educated Malawians, vernacular language means Chichewa, not English. The availability of the Bible in Chichewa translation is foundational to reducing barriers to understanding, and making its original message accessible to people in provincial-rural Malawi.

b) Chichewa Translations

There are two main Chichewa translations in Malawi used within the Protestant church.[1] The *Buku Lopatulika* (Sacred Book) was the product of Western expatriate missionary endeavour (Wendland 1998, 20–25). First published in 1922, its text is essentially unchanged today, though many of its words are no longer commonly used. It has a stilted verbal style analogous to that of the KJV in English. Its subtitle *ndilo Mau a Mulungu* (it is the Words of

---

1. Both are published by the Bible Society of Malawi. There is also an early Roman Catholic translation *Malembo Oyera*, not discussed.

God) might imply it is the complete equal of the original Hebrew and Greek, making it hard to substitute with a new Chichewa translation.

The *Buku Loyera* is a recent (1998) inter-church translation offering a more idiomatic, popular language version, almost a paraphrase. Its target audience is young adults with late primary level education and basic Christian knowledge (Wendland 1998, 74). Its mother-tongue translators prioritized dynamic equivalence over word-for-word translation, the unit of thought over the individual verse, and meaning over form (Wendland 1998, 26–47). The translators intentionally avoided inclusion of terms which they felt likely to be misunderstood (Wendland 1998, 45).

c)   Which Bible Translation is Used?

Many rural church leaders in Malawi have no access to a Bible or lack the literacy skills to read it. Chichewa Bible distribution partnered with literacy education must therefore remain a priority of Christian mission in rural Malawi.

Buku Lopatulika is popular with all the Protestant denominations in Malawi. It was used exclusively by the church leaders in this research, both the delegates at the training conferences and those taking part in Contextual Bible studies. Bible distribution policies by Christian missions have consistently promoted this version. It transports major theological themes from the Greek text into Chichewa with technical precision, and necessitates use of fewer words than *Loyera* to express ideas.[2]

Buku Loyera might appear to be a more suitable version for rural pastors with only basic general education, limited Chichewa vocabulary and little or no theological training. But *Buku Loyera* has not found widespread acceptance in the Malawian Protestant church over the past decade. *Buku Lopatulika* will remain the accepted translation, irrespective of whether it is always the most appropriate for understanding and contextualizing Scripture in rural churches. Continuing use of *Buku Lopatulika*, but perhaps making occasional cross reference to *Buku Loyera*, may offer a positive practical way to increase familiarity with and critical acceptance of this second translation.

---

2. For example, 3:21–26 requires 147 words in *Loyera*, but uses only 95 words in *Lopatulika*.